D0843210

# A GENEROSITY OF SPIRIT

# A GENEROSITY OF SPIRIT

## *The Early History of the Research Triangle Park*

### ALBERT N. LINK

PUBLISHED BY
THE RESEARCH TRIANGLE
FOUNDATION OF NORTH CAROLINA

Written permission to quote from this text, other than in critical articles,
reviews, and histories of the Research Triangle Park may be obtained by
writing to the Research Triangle Foundation, P.O. Box 12255, Research
Triangle Park, NC 27709.

Library of Congress Cataloging-in-Publication Data

Link, Albert N.
    A generosity of spirit : the early history of the Research Triangle Park /
    Albert N. Link.
        p.   cm.
    Includes bibliographical references and index.
    ISBN 0-9648051-0-3 (alk. paper)
    1. Research Triangle Park (N.C.)—History.    2. Research parks—North
Carolina—History.    3. Research institutes—North Carolina—History.
4. Research, Industrial—North Carolina—History.    I. Title.
Q180.6.U452R485    1995
338.9'75606—dc20                                            95-37943
                                                                CIP

Design by Suzanne Holt
Production by B. Williams & Associates

Printed on acid-free paper.  ∞

# CONTENTS

# ILLUSTRATIONS

# ACKNOWLEDGMENTS

Although neither born nor raised in North Carolina, I have developed a tremendous sense of pride in the state as a result of researching and writing this early history of the Research Triangle Park. As Archie Davis said many times, "There is something special about the people of North Carolina. For it was their love for the state that was the motivation for Research Triangle Park, and it was their generosity of spirit that made the Triangle the success that it is today."

I am thankful to a number of individuals for the opportunity to have a small part in the ongoing history of the Park. First, I am appreciative to the members of the Research Triangle Foundation Board, who entrusted me with the responsibility of writing this early history. Second, many individuals were generous enough to spend time with me recalling events that they were a part of some thirty or forty years ago. While my interviews with each of them are referenced at the end of the book, several individuals should be noted by name because they were kind enough to devote hours, and sometimes days, to reading many of the earlier versions of this manuscript and answering question after question. These include John Caldwell, Archie Davis, George Herbert, Bill Little, Bill Newell, John Sanders, George Simpson, and especially Elizabeth Aycock. Not enough can be said about my appreciation for the knowledge, time, and patience Elizabeth Aycock extended to me in seeing this project to completion. She exemplifies the generosity of spirit about which Archie Davis speaks. Third, there are my wife, Carol; daughter, Jamie; and son, Kevin, who, through their love and patience, were supportive throughout this project.

# FOREWORD

Albert Link has done a very important service in recording and interpreting historically significant events in this valuable and interesting volume on the emergence of the Research Triangle of North Carolina.

It is of particular importance that this work carefully identifies and underscores the immensely significant story of this period of our history: the union of effort among corporate leaders, government officers, and faculty and administrative leaders of these universities to create a unique and most successful enterprise of the highest quality—an enterprise that has elevated the appreciation of and respect for basic and applied research throughout the country.

Many individuals deserve credit and recognition for this success story. I am very glad that among others, Dr. Link has stressed the critical roles played by George Simpson, the architect of much that is lasting of those early years of struggle, and of George Herbert, Marcus Hobbs, Watts Hill, William Newell, A. C. Menius, Jr., William Little, and Gertrude Cox.

No story of the Triangle would be complete without a narration of the splendid leadership of Archie Davis. North Carolina has a great tradition of public service, so long the hallmark of its leaders throughout the history of the state. There is no finer manifestation of that tradition than the splendid service Archie Davis has given his state, especially in building the Research Triangle, as Dr. Link has written.

Special note must be made, too, of the great skill of Elizabeth Aycock, who kept the organizational processes on the proper course and, in her own way, brought the many ideas and actions together into a consistent record of achievement and progress.

Dr. Link gives the reader an interesting and instructive journey through a very special interval of North Carolina history. He makes clear that the flowering of the Triangle has certainly changed the course of the state's development in the latter half of the twentieth century and put North Carolina firmly into the global community of major research centers.

Dr. Link merits high praise for giving all of us such a valuable history and a highly readable account of this remarkable achievement by a citizenry long known for its creative spirit and its willingness to adventure into new relationships.

WILLIAM FRIDAY
*Chapel Hill, North Carolina*

# A GENEROSITY OF SPIRIT

# The Research Triangle Area

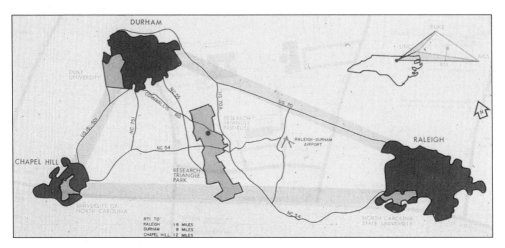

Circa early 1960s

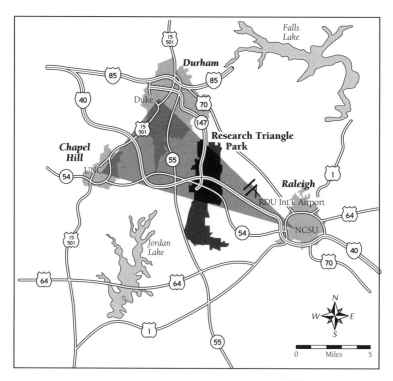

1995

# INTRODUCTION

*Progress is the activity of today and the assurance of tomorrow.*
—RALPH WALDO EMERSON

## WHAT IS THE RESEARCH TRIANGLE?

"In the heart of North Carolina there exists one of the Nation's most important industrial resources . . . the Research Triangle."[1]

Over the past thirty years, the term "Research Triangle" has been used in a number of different ways. When it was first used in the early 1950s, before any formal organization had been proposed or any land acquired,[2] the term referred to the general area defined by the three academic institutions: the University of North Carolina at Chapel Hill, North Carolina State College in Raleigh,[3] and Duke University in Durham.

Former governor Luther H. Hodges (1954–61), one of the early champions of the Triangle concept, thought of the Research Triangle (as it existed in 1962) in slightly broader terms:

> Research Triangle should be thought of as basically three things. First it is an actual tract of land—the five thousand-acre Research Triangle park spread over the beautiful central Carolina countryside, which a decade ago was empty pineland and where now a half-dozen laboratories and research buildings are a promise of even more to come. Second, the Research Triangle is the larger area surrounding the park,

triangular in shape, with corners at Raleigh, Durham, and Chapel Hill—the homes of three of North Carolina's greatest institutions of higher education, North Carolina State College, Duke University, and the University of North Carolina. Finally and most important, the Research Triangle is an idea that has produced a reality—the idea that the brains and talents of the three institutions, and their life of research in many fields, could provide the background and stimulation of research for the benefit of the State and Nation. In a way, the Research Triangle is the marriage of North Carolina's ideals for higher education and its hopes for material progress. (Hodges 1962, p. 203)

In its earliest time, the popular press also thought of the Research Triangle in a multifaceted as well as forward-looking manner. To quote from "The Meaning of the Research Triangle," an article that appeared in the *Winston-Salem Journal-Sentinel* on December 18, 1964,

What is the Research Triangle? . . . There is no simple answer because the Research Triangle is many things. . . . It is a place, a geographical location. It is both an idea and a practical concept. It is a triad of operating institutions, interlaced with both private and public interests and support, and with three great universities at its cornerstones. . . . It is also a physical reality, a center of research in science and technology, something which has become a complex of new landscaped buildings, modern offices and gleaming laboratories.

Today Research Triangle Park is a well-defined area of 6,800 acres within a scalene triangle formed by the three universities. Within its incorporated boundaries, more than seventy research organizations, employing over 34,000 individuals, form a complex entity for the sharing of ideas. As it did in the beginning, this collection of public and private enterprises now represents an assurance of tomorrow for the State of North Carolina.

### AN ASSURANCE OF TOMORROW

After World War II, the North Carolina economy was very unstable. Historically, the state's economy had relied almost exclusively on three traditional industries: furniture, textiles, and tobacco. The furniture industry was leaving the state and expanding into the northeastern United States; the textile industry was beginning to face growing competition from Asian producers; and tobacco manufacturing employment was on the decline, due in part to automation and in part to decreasing demand, which resulted from publicity about tobacco as a potential cause of cancer. Not only did it have a precarious economic base; in addition, North Carolina's per capita income had long been one of the lowest in the nation. In fact, North Carolina was losing its ability to employ its own college graduates: its best students were attracted to the industrial opportunities that were increasing in other regions of the country.

There was thus a need to diversify and expand the state's economy. According to Elizabeth J. Aycock (1991), the only individual who has continued to be associated with the Research Triangle since its formal inception, "The simple reason for the creation of the concept that has made the Research Triangle was to diversify the economy. The other most important reason was to reverse the brain drain—the outmigration of our young people."

The business, industrial, and educational leaders of the time saw Research Triangle Park as a means of guiding the state into a "future of industrial development" (Hodges 1962, p. 204): "The heart and hope of North Carolina's industrial future is the Research Triangle. . . . The Research Triangle [Park] offers North Carolina an assurance of tomorrow, but only if we remember that progress is the activity of today" (Hodges 1962, pp. 203, 223).

Without question, Research Triangle Park has been an unequaled effort in economic development, providing both employment opportunities and international visibility for the state as a whole. It is known by name throughout the world; it welcomes over five thousand visitors each year; it has contributed to the growth and diversity of the state's economy over the past three decades; and it has strengthened the academic reputations and resource bases of the three universities: "The Triangle has created an environment, a research environment . . . that could not have existed the way it does now. This is an international crossroads. Every scientist [in the world] knows what the Research Triangle is" (Little 1992).

The history of Research Triangle Park can be told in a number of ways. One could simply chronicle the key events. For example, in the early 1950s, the idea reemerged that the three academic institutions could act as a magnet to attract research companies to North Carolina. The location of research companies would lead to the development of new industry, and new industry would in turn spur the state's waning economic base. Once persuaded of the economic development merits of this idea, Governor Hodges appointed a committee of university and corporate leaders to refine the concept. As this committee was working, private investors were assembling land within the triangle formed by the three institutions. This land (about four thousand acres) would eventually become known as Research Triangle Park. Realizing that Research Triangle Park would benefit the entire state and that funds for its development could only come through donations given for the good of the state, Archie Davis led a statewide effort to raise money to acquire the previously assembled land and to establish the nonprofit Research Triangle Foundation. After a number of years of very slow growth, the Park received commitments from three major tenants in 1965. Since then, the Park's growth has represented one of the most successful economic development efforts in the postwar period.

Unfortunately, such a simple chronicling of historical events grossly understates the real history of Research Triangle Park. To understand why the Park was successful, one must understand the character of the individuals who unselfishly gave of their time, talents, and money for the common good of the State of North Carolina. It was this generosity of spirit and mind that is the history of Research Triangle Park.

## WHY WAS RESEARCH TRIANGLE PARK A SUCCESS?

Visitors to the Park ask James O. Roberson, the president of the Research Triangle Foundation, one question more often than any other: "What can we do to develop a park like this?" Others have tried, but few have succeeded in matching the economic development success of the Triangle.

Why was Research Triangle Park a success? There were three factors: one, the location of three universities; two, the citizenry of North Carolina; and three, timing and luck. No one of these ingredients would have been sufficient; no one of these factors is more important than another; all three were critical for ensuring the long-term success of the Park.

## The Universities

It is rare for a state or region to have three outstanding universities clustered together. In the early 1950s, North Carolina's Triangle institutions contained two medical schools, two engineering schools, and a core of preeminent researchers in nearly every field of science. And within these institutions were some "bold thinkers"—a blend of individuals with backgrounds that could initiate cooperation among the institutions (Caldwell 1991).

The Research Triangle concept carried with it the "implication that the three institutions could act, in appropriate instances, as a unified academic and research community" (Hobbs 1982). They had a long history of serving the state independently—Chapel Hill in education and government, State College in agriculture, and Duke in medicine (Simpson 1993c). It is not natural for universities to gravitate toward institutional solutions of institutional problems. One special element that spurred cooperation among the three universities in this project was Governor Hodges, who offered both leadership and respect for the academic mission of the universities (Simpson 1957b).[4]

The idea of university cooperation in research was not new. Howard W. Odum, professor of sociology at the University of North Carolina at Chapel Hill and founder (in 1924) of the Institute for Research in Social Science, was an early proponent of research cooperation between the universities in Raleigh and Chapel Hill.[5] In 1952, Odum proposed several research center formats. Each was designed to draw on the humanities and social science expertise of these two institutions in the University of North Carolina system. Although they were never funded, these proposals certainly influenced the thinking of administrators toward the general idea of research cooperation.

To make the situation even more favorable, the three institutions were located near a major airport and railway system, and the Sunbelt location was gaining in national popularity because of its quality of life.

### The Citizenry of North Carolina

Archibald ("Archie") K. Davis—the primary fund-raiser and leader of the Park in the early years—places a great emphasis on the importance of the citizenry of North Carolina for the success of the Research Triangle. People in North Carolina, he says, work together for the good of the state: "I am convinced that it is the love of this state that was the motivation for the Research Triangle idea. Motivation derives from dedication and dedication derives from the knowledge of high expectations. . . . Research Triangle is a manifestation of what North Carolina is all about" (Davis 1992).

People in North Carolina have long exhibited a statewide perspective. In the 1950s and 1960s there was no dominant city in North Carolina. There were regional political differences, of course, but these differences fed into a strong statewide perspective. Philanthropists had a tradition of showing attention to the state as a whole. North Carolina formed its first state symphony in the 1930s and its first state art museum in the 1950s (Vogel 1985). Such efforts for the good of the state also helped to form a close leadership structure.

George Simpson, a student of southern society, traces the North Carolina tradition of commitment and involvement in the state as a whole to the post–Civil War period:

> After the War, North Carolina and the South in general, went through a period of self-doubt and re-evaluation. During this time, people probably tended to retreat back among themselves, depending on their own small circle of acquaintances, for nearly all of their social interaction. They eventually formed various groups and organizations, and spent nearly all their time together—whether it was in business or social activities. They got to know one another very well, and were constantly communicating with one another.   (Franco 1985, p. 223)

Here, according to Simpson, is the seed of North Carolina's tradition of interaction.

### Timing and Luck

The timing for Research Triangle Park was fortunate. Many business leaders had learned during World War II that research was a critical element for industrial growth. New industries were developing, and many of them needed new and improved technologies. Route 128 around Boston and the Stanford Research Institute in California were attracting national attention. In addition, Sputnik was launched in 1957, and this event christened the space agency as a major competitor with industry for doctoral scientists. In the mid- to late 1950s there was a tremendous shortage of Ph.D.'s. Industry relished the thought of having access to the supply of scientists from nearby universities (Little 1992). The time seemed right for the idea of a research park.

Having the idea was one thing; seeing it to a successful end was another. North Carolina enjoyed some luck in this matter. The brain drain, one factor that partially influenced the initial thinking about an economic development strategy for the state, also put many North Carolinians in positions of prominence within major research corporations in the Northeast. These individuals were naturally receptive to a North Carolina project, and they already knew firsthand about the quality of life in the state.

It was also a matter of some luck that North Carolina elected two dynamic and tireless governors during critical stages of the Park's development—Luther Hodges (1954–61) and Terry Sanford (1961–65). Hodges was able to provide the initial organizational spark to get the project going in the mid-1950s. Sanford was able to capitalize on his political connections in Washington to influence the decision of at least one key tenant to locate in Research Triangle Park.

It took a special blending of these factors—the universities, the state's citizenry, and timing and luck—to create the momentum necessary to produce Research Triangle Park. Whether it could have happened elsewhere, or whether it can happen again, are questions that will continue to be debated. The fact of the matter is that it did happen in North Carolina and that it was successful.

According to Davis (1992), "There's something about North Carolina that I think is unmatched anywhere in the country." In North Carolina, there is a "generosity of spirit" and a "generosity of mind"[6]—people work together for the common good of the state, as one can see from the history of the Research Triangle Park.[7]

# CHAPTER 1

# THE IDEA TAKES SHAPE

*I would have all our people believe their power to accomplish
as much as can be done anywhere on earth by any people.*
— CHARLES B. AYCOCK
*Governor of North Carolina, 1901–5*

## SETTING THE STAGE

Brandon P. Hodges (no relationship to Governor Luther Hodges) was elected the state treasurer of North Carolina in November 1948. One of his goals was to bring new types of industry, particularly technology-based industries, into the state. According to Paul M. Gross, vice president of Duke University during the initial stages of the Park's planning, "The fact was that in North Carolina in the 1950s, there was very little industrial research and development going on anywhere, even though it was recognized elsewhere as important to the overall economy. With the problems we were facing in our existing industries, it was clear that we needed to get a piece of the pie as well" (Franco 1985, p. 157).

No one was thinking about abandoning the traditional industries of furniture, textiles, and tobacco. Rather, people were justifiably concerned that the state's economy needed to diversify in order to grow. And there was indeed room for growth.

According to William F. Little, professor of chemistry at the University of North Carolina at Chapel Hill and an early participant in the activities of the Research Triangle, "We were pretty much in a rut back [in the early 1950s]. We saw that other places were starting to make progress in other types of business that involved some of the new technology. But we had little activity along those lines. We were, and still are, a heavily agricultural state. The idea behind the Park was not so much that we'd try to throw away our traditional industries, but that we'd attempt to get more diversity" (Franco 1985, p. 210).

Data from the U.S. Department of Commerce show that in 1950 only five states in the nation had a per capita income level lower than North Carolina's. By 1952, only two states did—Arkansas and Mississippi. For that same year, per capita income in North Carolina was $1,049, compared to $1,121 for the eleven-state Southeast region as a whole and $1,639 for the continental United States (Spivey 1956, pp. 19, 21).

In addition, North Carolina was heavily dependent on the agricultural sector. In 1951, over 17 percent of the state's income came directly from agriculture; this percentage was exceeded in the Southeast only by that in Arkansas and Mississippi. In 1950, there were 289,000 farms in North Carolina, a total second only to that in Texas. The average size of each of these farms was only 67 acres—the lowest in the nation. The average farm size in the South was 148 acres, and for the nation it was 216 acres. Then, as today, it was difficult for small-sized farms to justify the cost associated with new farming technology.

In the early 1950s, a number of academic and industrial groups in North Carolina were thinking seriously about economic development in general, and, in particular, how the universities could help attract industry to the state.[1] State College, for example, had a long history of interacting with industry. In the early 1950s, J. Harold Lampe, dean of the School of Engineering at State College, established industry-focused continuing education courses under the engineering extension service. On that campus and elsewhere there was a growing awareness of the potential mutual benefits associated with industry-university relationships, and people were beginning to think seriously about the universities as an important economic resource.[2]

The idea of a state's university structure being used as a key element in an economic development plan was not new. North Carolina governor R. Gregg Cherry (1945–49) made this specific point at a 1945 conference on research and regional welfare at the University of North

Carolina at Chapel Hill: "North Carolina and the South for many years lagged in scientific research and in the application of the results of research to industry. . . . Not only must we locate the industries in the South, but we must also have the research laboratories that improve these industries, and by that means improve also our people and their way of life" (Cherry 1946, pp. 5–6). Robert E. Coker, Kenan Professor of Zoology at the University of North Carolina at Chapel Hill, also spoke at this conference:

> Beyond any possible question, the fountainhead of both theoretical and applied research is in universities. It is only there that one finds the diversity of skills and the broad freedom of analysis that must be brought to bear on special problems of all sorts. It is only there that the essential personnel for research can be primarily selected and given the basic training to produce competence in practical research. It is chiefly in universities that the solid foundation of fundamental or so-called "pure" research can be laid. After all, it is the facts and the ideas of fundamental research that keep filling the reservoir into which the industrial researcher inevitably must dip. (Coker 1946, p. xiv)

## ROMEO GUEST

### Who Was Romeo Guest?

Walter Harper, who was involved with Romeo Guest and the Triangle concept early on in his capacity with the Department of Conservation and Development (C&D),[3] reflected, "In my estimation, there is no one person that conceived the Research Triangle or was exclusively responsible for it happening. But there were a series of involvements, and I felt that the concept tended to take on a life as it went along, and many people made major contributions" (Harper 1991). George Simpson exhibited this same viewpoint in a 1957 speech before the University of North Carolina Faculty Club: "I do not know if it is possible to identify *the* [emphasis added] person through whom the idea of the Research Triangle first came into being" (Simpson 1957b, p. 1). Although she was not involved until 1956, Elizabeth Aycock (1991) noted that the Park has developed this way since its inception: "The interesting thing is that there were two or three people involved here, two or three people involved over there . . . and things came together. That's been the case over the years." According to Harper, though, "Romeo [Guest] had the single largest part in bringing the idea to fruition, but it could not have happened without the others who were involved. . . . He didn't make the football, but he sure carried it a long way down the field. . . . Romeo was the leader of the band; no question about it" (Harper 1992).[4]

While there are differing opinions as to Guest's role in the conceptualization of the Research Triangle idea, it is clear that Governor Hodges, while publicly taking much of the credit for the Research Triangle, noted in personal correspondence to Guest that "we have not forgotten that it was your idea" (letter dated December 6, 1956) and that "you are really the person that gave birth to the idea of the Research Triangle. You deserve much of the credit" (letter dated November 17, 1959).

The economic growth potential of the burgeoning research industry was not new to Guest. As an observant student, he had firsthand knowledge of how industries were congregating around the research laboratories at Harvard and MIT. He also saw this phenomenon occurring nearby, though to a lesser degree.[5]

In 1939, Guest met with executives of Merck and Company, Inc.[6] Henry W. Johnstone, vice president for administration, discussed with Guest Merck's plan for a production facility in the South.[7] As it turned out, North Carolina did not offer any location that was both close to the coast and near an ample supply of groundwater for cooling the chemical reactions. The production facility was eventually built in Elkton, Virginia (Guest 1977). According to Guest, "The people at Merck thought the close proximity [to the University of Virginia] would reduce turnover among their scientists and other highly paid people. So I saw [firsthand] that research encouraged more research and manufacturing" (Colvard 1986, p. 5). Guest was given a contract to construct the Elkton plant. Afterward he visited the corporation's headquarters in Rahway, New Jersey, and many years later he recalled that he realized then that research was an industry unto itself (Guest 1977).

In the late 1940s and early 1950s, Guest remained in close contact with individuals at C&D in Raleigh. He thought that if he could be involved in helping a company locate a site and move to North Carolina, he would have an inside track on building its facility (Harper 1991). It had always been Guest's practice not to bid on construction contracts. If he did not receive a noncompetitive contract, he simply did not become involved. Without question, Guest was a profit-oriented business man, but he also had a sense of public spirit (Little 1992).

In the early 1950s, at his own expense, Guest traveled along the East Coast with Brandon Hodges and Walter Harper in search of companies that might relocate in North Carolina.[8] Harper recalled that Guest knew a number of corporate leaders and that he would introduce him to them on their trips.[9]

Although Guest was a shrewd business man, there was also a lighter side to his personality. On one occasion, according to Harper (1991),

> We had a prospect in York, Pennsylvania . . . York Wire Company or some kind of wire company. . . . I told Romeo I'd been talking to the president of the company and he says he's got to have a good financial package, so Romeo brought in a financial man from New York and we all met the prospect in York, and everything just went fine. They wanted to put the plant in Southern Pines. . . . Everything was just perfect. We got back to the hotel, [and] I said, "We've got this one; let's go have a party."
>
> Romeo, he was a great personality; he didn't look the part; he looked so serious, and so very much like he could have been a professor! He had a great . . . spirit and loved a party. And I said, "Romeo, we got this plant, now let's go out and celebrate."
>
> He said, "Walter, suppose we don't get the plant? Suppose something happens and we don't get it?"
>
> And I said, "Hell, then at least we'll have a party!"
>
> Sure enough, we went out and we had a nice meal and a real party; went to this club somewhere down in York, Pennsylvania. I don't know how we found a club there. . . . Sure enough, something

happened to the company, not anything we had [done]. . . . I used to laugh at Romeo after that. I'd say, "Well, we didn't get the plant but we had a hell of a good party!"

During this time period—between 1951 and 1953—Brandon Hodges, Harper, and Guest would continue to discuss what could be done to attract industry to North Carolina [10] and how the state could take better advantage of its enormous resources in education (Wilson 1967; Harper 1991).[11] Harper recalled, "Romeo Guest, Brandon Hodges and I talked over the importance and relationship of research to industrial and economic development of the State on many occasions in 1952 and 1953. These discussions were related to and stimulated by a number of industrial prospects on which we were *all* [emphasis added] working during that period. Some of the discussions took place in Raleigh; others in New York and throughout the State on our industrial promotional trips" (Harper 1960).

What was missing from these early discussions was a means of relating the state's educational resources to its economic development needs. Although the exact mechanism was missing, a number of individuals at the time began to articulate that the proximity of the three Triangle universities could be used as a magnet to attract research companies.[12]

In an April 26, 1981 interview with the *Durham Morning Herald*, Guest recalled, "It was 10 A.M. on December 31, 1954. I was with Gov. Hodges and I looked at a map and noticed that the universities formed a triangle." Though this recollection of the naming of the Triangle area is appealing, it is inaccurate.[13] The term "Research Triangle," referring to the general area formed by the three universities—the University of North Carolina at Chapel Hill, State College, and Duke University— appeared to have been used by Guest as early as 1952. John L. Ponzer of Southern Pines, North Carolina, wrote to Charles Jeffries of the *Raleigh News and Observer* on March 3, 1983, in response to an article about the Research Triangle, particularly to its inaccurate portrayal of Governor Hodges as the author of the concept:

> Romeo Guest and I were having a drink one afternoon before a Carolina Power and Light Co. meeting at the [Richmond County] Country Club [in Rockingham in the early 1950s]. We were discuss-

ing some infrared heating tests being conducted at Duke University. I distinctly remember making the following remark: "With all the technical know how and research at N.C. State Schools of Engineering and Textiles plus Duke's Engineering School it appears that they would find a way to dry a string that had been immersed in a starch solution (textile warp) as few things are impossible these days with research."

Romeo replied: "I agree and I am glad to know your feelings as I have been giving some thought to a similar idea. We need a Research Center to help the textile boys."

We then discussed the possibilities of a joint venture by Duke and State. We also discussed the possibilities of including Carolina and Wake Forest [Wake Forest University, now located in Winston-Salem, was originally located in Wake Forest, North Carolina]. We finally agreed that Duke, Carolina and State offered the greatest potential and could be called the Research Triangle Center.

A brown paper bag on which Ponzer and Guest later sketched the location of this center shows it surrounded by the four institutions (Aycock 1993). On this bag they also jotted five possible names, including "Research Triangle Park."

On September 8, 1952, Phyllis Branch Case recorded in her daybook (an expense account diary) a payment to Bill Crawford for aerial photographs of the Triangle area around the Raleigh-Durham airport (Case 1991a). Walter Harper and William P. Saunders, director of C&D under Governor Hodges, also recalled Guest talking about the Research Triangle as early as 1952 (Harper 1960; Guest 1980).[14] In a June 8, 1953 recruiting letter to William A. Bunney, vice president of E. R. Squibb and Sons, Guest made a general reference to the area surrounded by the three universities.[15] Then, in a July 15, 1953 follow-up letter to Bruce Hainsworth, director of engineering at Squibb, Guest mentioned an upcoming visit to the company by Brandon Hodges and expressed his hope that Squibb would consider North Carolina because of "our research area at Durham, Chapel Hill, and Raleigh." Also, Guest's diary for October 10, 1953, contains this notation for a meeting with Brandon Hodges and Robert Armstrong, director of research at Celanese Corporation: "Research Triangle—Celanese."[16]

There seems to be no doubt in the minds of many of the individuals who were active in the development of the Research Triangle that Guest deserves full credit for the "phraseology" of the Research Triangle (Davis 1992). According to Aycock (1991), "Romeo Guest really put Research Triangle, those two words, together."

However, in a February 5, 1955 correspondence from Harris Purks, vice president and provost of the Consolidated University of North Carolina, to Gordon Gray, president of the Consolidated University, Purks offered Gray several comments on the Campbell and Newell report (discussed below), including this one: "As long as five [years] ago the words 'The Carolina Triangle' were used in conversations among officers in our national foundation to designate the unusual educational facilities existing in the Raleigh-Durham-Chapel Hill area."

The Triangle idea was simple; the three universities would act as a magnet to attract research companies into the area, and this in turn would lead to the development of new industries throughout the state.

I hesitate to attribute exclusive credit to Guest for the idea of using the three universities to attract research industries to the state; clearly, the general concept was already being discussed by Harper, Brandon Hodges, Guest, and, in all probability, others as well. In fact, this theme had been discussed at the May 1945 conference on research and regional welfare at the University of North Carolina at Chapel Hill.[17]

It is also important to note that there are those who disagree with this proposition. According to Case,

> There is no doubt in my mind that Romeo Guest was the one who originally conceived the idea of establishing a place in North Carolina where the research atmosphere was conducive for firms to engage in basic and applied research. He thought the natural result from basic and applied research would spark industry to locate nearby for a two-prong growth effect for the state. Romeo Guest was cognizant of the economic condition of North Carolina in the late forties and early fifties and knew that since the movement of industries to the southeast was past its peak, a new basis for growth must be found in order to keep our young graduates home and to form a viable tax base for the state. (Case 1991b)

Without a doubt, Guest himself would agree with Case. In fact, he was noted as saying, "*I* [emphasis added] was trying to promote the idea of getting research here to develop new products, and then have satellite plants produce the product. I said that what we would do would be to hatch our own industries, and then we would have them build their production facilities in our outlying towns. The concept was to separate the thinking from the hammering" (Franco 1985, p. 95). Perhaps Harper (1992) is correct: "[Guest] didn't make the football, but he sure carried it a long way down the field."

## SELLING THE RESEARCH TRIANGLE IDEA

A luncheon meeting took place on March 3, 1954, at the Robert E. Lee Hotel in Winston-Salem, North Carolina, between Brandon Hodges; Robert M. Hanes, president of Wachovia Bank and Trust Company; and Romeo Guest.[18] The purpose of this meeting was to discuss North Carolina's need for industrial growth. However, Guest took advantage of this opportunity to explain to Hanes the Research Triangle idea, with which Brandon Hodges was already familiar. In addition to explaining the concept, Guest presented Hanes with a list of individuals who perhaps could help develop the idea. The list was titled "Suggested Industrial Committee," and Hanes was the suggested chairman (Guest 1977; Jones 1978).[19]

According to Case (1960), who probably was told firsthand about this meeting, "Mr. Hanes listened carefully to the idea but was not immediately 'sold.' His enthusiastic leadership came about a year later. Mr. Hanes' early reaction was that each industry [company] would want its [research] laboratory near its factory."

That fall, having had time to contemplate the idea, Hanes suggested to Brandon Hodges that he set up a meeting for Guest to discuss the Research Triangle idea with Governor William B. Umstead (1953–54).[20] In an October 12, 1954 letter from Hanes to Guest, it appeared that this meeting never took place, due to the governor's illness (Guest 1977). Governor Umstead died in office on November 7, 1954, and was succeeded by Lieutenant Governor Luther Hodges.[21]

Also in the fall of 1954,[22] after returning to State College as assistant director of foundations, Harper shared the Triangle idea with his colleagues Malcolm E. Campbell, dean of textiles; Harold Lampe, dean of engineering; and William A. Newell, director of the Textile Research Center.

Newell remembered that in Campbell's office, Guest showed the men a pasted-up version of his advertising pamphlet, "Conditioned for Research." Newell's reaction to the concept was that "there would have to be a park"[23] (Newell 1992). Newell (1989) pointed out that "such an area could not only provide a 'campus' atmosphere for individual research laboratories but support facilities needed to undergird research, such as service or testing laboratories." Newell (1989, 1992) recalled that a few days after this meeting he took out a map of North Carolina, traced the triangle formed by the three institutions, and sketched in the principal roads. He shaded in a parklike square and sent the tracing to Guest with a note that said, "Romeo, how's this? Bill."

Newell (1992) does not remember if the area that he shaded actually turned out to be near the Park as we know it today. His purpose in making the sketch was only to illustrate to Guest the park concept. Guest (1976, 1977) recalled the map in a later interview and thought that he received it sometime in January 1955. According to Harper (1991), it was somewhat ironic that he and Guest missed the park idea, given that both of them were site location men, and that it was Newell —a concept person—who focused immediately on its importance.

The first time Carey H. Bostian, chancellor at State College, learned about the Research Triangle idea was when he received a telephone call from Malcolm Campbell.[24] Campbell told him that he had an idea he would like to present to Governor Hodges.[25]

On December 1, 1954, Bostian, Campbell, Lampe, and Brandon Hodges met with Governor Hodges to inform him of the Research Triangle idea.[26] According to Bostian, the governor "did not show a great deal of enthusiasm" for the idea, but he was polite (Bostian 1991). Interestingly, the governor later wrote that the idea of the Research Triangle was mentioned to him in early 1955 by Brandon Hodges, "and immediately I saw the potential it held for North Carolina" (Hodges 1962).

According to John T. Caldwell (1991), who followed Bostian as chancellor at State College, "Luther Hodges did not establish the Research Triangle Park. . . . They had to talk Luther Hodges into this" (Caldwell 1991). Newell (1992) agrees that Hodges did not at first understand the Research Triangle idea; he notes that the governor had a textile background and did not understand the nature of research and development.

After the December 1 meeting, the governor requested that Bostian prepare an objective assessment of the idea of a research park in North Carolina of the type proposed. Newell, who had long been a student of research and development in the textile industry, was asked to prepare the report. "A Proposal for the Development of an Industrial Research Center in North Carolina" was written during Newell's Christmas vacation. Newell added Campbell's name to it, because Campbell was the one who would have to approve it before it went to Bostian.[27]

The ten-page report contains some interesting observations:

> This proposal does not express a new idea. Rather, it outlines broadly an idea that has existed in the minds of many[28] North Carolina leaders for some time.   (p. i)

> The State of North Carolina today has unique and undeveloped advantages that can attract research organizations to the State and that can lead to the development of an important research center of the United States. The growth of research organizations within the State can, in turn, lead to the attraction of existing industries to the State and the development of new industries within the State.   (p. ii)

> Specific plans should be made for the development of an area between Raleigh, Durham and Chapel Hill and near Raleigh-Durham Airport, as a center for industrial research.   (p. 9)[29]

> Plans for the actual development including financing of the area should be made.   (p. 10)

> The colleges and universities involved should be apprised of the plans and encouraged to consider their place in them and establish and make known policies concerning this place.   (p. 10)

In retrospect, Newell's report was a remarkable blueprint; the activities that followed over the next decade mirror his suggestions. Newell (1992) believes, and I agree, that he was the first person to articulate in writing the concept of encouraging research and development organizations to locate near the universities. Bostian sent the final report to Governor Hodges on January 27, 1955.[30]

Campbell remembered having lunch with Governor Hodges three Tuesdays in a row after the governor had received the Campbell-Newell report (Guest 1976). According to Campbell, Harper and Guest were also present at these meetings (Guest 1976). It was not until the third meeting, as Campbell recalled, that the governor began to understand and buy into the idea.[31] Thereafter, the idea became "the governor's Research Triangle."

According to Campbell, the governor did not take him seriously at the first meeting:

> He kind of joked along with what I was trying to paint as a serious picture how we would get a pamphlet out, survey the area, get it out, and put all sorts of things in it. And he called me a huckster! And you don't say, "Governor, you're a damn fool."
>
> You don't say that. I said, "Governor, is there such a thing as being a dignified huckster?"
>
> Well, he kind of laughed it off for two luncheons. Then at the third luncheon, he bought the thing right then and there. He bought the thing, and from there on out, it was the Governor's Research Triangle.   (Guest 1976)

Those involved with these sporadic events and meetings may have misinterpreted the governor's reaction to the Research Triangle idea. Governor Hodges concentrated intensely on industrial development from day one:

> He [the governor] was moving in every direction. He staked his reputation on [industrial development]. His reception of the Triangle idea [should be] properly seen in that context. . . . It was sometimes easy to underestimate the Governor. One reason was as follows. On one day on a subject, he might appear all superficial, even inattentive. The next day on the same subject he would be both fundamental and hard working. He thought ahead on implementation very fast, at the moment of understanding the concept; I think he saw obstacles to be surmounted very quickly, and took time to think about those matters before saying much. Also, he disciplined his work severely, being almost obsessed with finishing a job, or at least taking a step. He may have had other things on his mind, originally. I'd be surprised if his first thoughts on the Triangle were not "how" rather than "what." And of course, "who."   (Simpson 1993b, 1993c)

During this time period, Guest continued to promote what he saw as an opportunity to position himself for future construction contracts. He did promote the Triangle idea with his own funds, but not without the explicit notice of his company.

He prepared a pamphlet entitled "Conditioned for Research."[32] The opening sentences in the pamphlet clearly state the Triangle concept as it existed in late 1954: "The Research Triangle of North Carolina today offers most unusual and favorable conditions for the location and operation of industrial research facilities. Far from crowded cities, limited equipment, and pressing personnel problems, industry will find in North Carolina a combination of living and working conditions—facilities and technical assistance—scientific experience and cooperation that creates an atmosphere . . . Conditioned for Research." The brochure describes the three academic institutions and the nearby technical assistance, scientific consultation, and trained personnel. According to Guest (Colvard 1986), the map that he put in the pamphlet was the one that gave him the idea for the name "Research Triangle." Figure 1 shows Guest's version of this map, used for his brochures.

The pamphlet clearly indicated the role that Guest saw for himself in the Research Triangle project: he hoped to become the contractor for the companies that located in the area. The C. M. Guest and Sons logo is prominent on the cover; the last paragraph stated that "C. M. Guest and Sons is playing its part in the motivation of the Research Triangle. We can answer questions and assist you in your planning. We invite you to write to us for detailed information."[33]

It was Guest's intention to use the pamphlet to advertise the Research Triangle and his company's services. However, at the urging of state senator Oscar Arthur Kirkman, Guest first made the Research Triangle idea known to the political and industrial leaders of the state. He sent a few letters to his closest friends for their comments. Mrs. Julius Cone of Greensboro received one of these letters, dated December 22, 1954. She urged Guest "not to get out on a limb by committing the University to something President Gray would not support" (Guest 1976).[34] The earliest version of "Conditioned for Research" suggested that the universities were able and willing to serve as consultants to industry (Guest 1977).

Other letters were mailed to prominent North Carolinians on

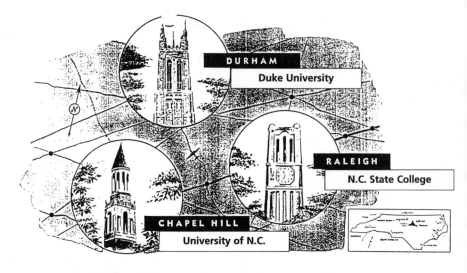

Figure 1. *The Research Triangle map first used by Romeo H. Guest.*

December 28, without the full text of the pamphlet. This one-page letter on C. M. Guest and Sons letterhead was primarily informative: "We have been sparking an idea with a small group of leaders and we want to tell you about it. We believe that by establishing here more laboratories for research and development of new products, the natural outgrowth will be the 'hatching of new industries' in North Carolina." Attached to this letter was a one-page flyer made up of material excerpted from "Conditioned for Research." The phrase "Research fits North Carolina like a glove" was featured prominently.

Brandon Hodges had been urging Guest to see Governor Hodges.[35] Guest did try to see him on December 20, 1954. Finally, he was able to make an appointment at 10:00 A.M. on December 31.[36] According to Guest, the governor was not very responsive to the Triangle idea at this meeting (Franco 1985).

That same afternoon Guest visited Gordon Gray, president of the University of North Carolina, and showed him "Conditioned for Research." Gray's response was favorable, and he said, according to

Guest, that he would support the idea as long as it did not interfere with the teaching mission of the university.[37]

During that last week of December 1954, Guest also visited Arthur Hollis Edens, president of Duke University.[38] Edens apparently liked the concept, because he promised to establish an ad hoc university committee to learn more about it (Guest 1977). This committee included Paul Gross, vice president; Marcus E. Hobbs, dean of the graduate school; and Walter J. Seeley, dean of engineering. Their first meeting with Guest was on January 4, 1955. At that meeting, Gross set forth his view that it would be crucial to have a research institute associated with the Park (Jones 1978).

By early January 1955, all of the critical players had been contacted and had agreed, in principle, that the Research Triangle idea had merit. It took until May 1955 for Guest to receive revisions for "Conditioned for Research" from the governor and university officials. In a note to Gordon Gray written between May 3 and May 10, William D. Carmichael, the university system's chief financial officer, offered his comments on the brochure in a typically succinct way: "I *guess* this is alright—no pun intended." Guest made his large mailing later that month (Jones 1978).

With most of the groundwork laid, it was time to take the first step.

# CHAPTER 2

# TAKING THE FIRST STEP

*Leadership and learning are indispensable to each other.*
—JOHN F. KENNEDY

FEBRUARY 9, 1955

Having contacted the relevant leaders at the three institutions, Romeo Guest continued to show state officials a pasted-up version of his "Conditioned for Research" brochure and to lay a foundation that would encourage new companies to locate in the area. In early January 1955, Guest contacted county commissioners R. J. M. Hobbs of Orange County, G. M. Kirkland of Durham County, and John P. Swain of Wake County. He proposed a tax relief program for new companies seeking to locate their research facilities in the general Triangle area. While these men acknowledged the logic of Guest's idea, Frank A. Pierson, executive vice president of the Durham Chamber of Commerce, opposed it (Jones 1978). Although no one realized it at the time, this would be only the first of many obstacles for the Park that would originate with Durham County.

The time that Guest spent with his letter campaign and the efforts that he expended to strike a compromise agreement with the universities on acceptable wording for "Conditioned for Research" showed him that the development of the Triangle concept was perhaps beyond his individual capabilities.[1] Actually, one oral record suggests that Guest always expected the state to become directly involved in the Research Triangle project.[2] Perhaps the state's involvement occurred earlier than he envisioned, but the time was now right for Governor Luther Hodges to step forward and exert his leadership.[3]

On January 30, 1955, Guest wrote directly to Governor Hodges: "It would appear that the time is right now for you to assume the leadership of the program, and to consider if advisable the establishment of an Advisory Council to the Research Triangle in order that advantage may be taken of the opportunities which are within our reach." Carey Bostian from State College also assumed a leadership position at this time (perhaps at Guest's urging through Walter Harper and Malcolm Campbell). He too urged the governor to become more active (Hamilton 1966).

The governor did become involved.[4] As reported by Bostian in a February 4, 1955, letter to Guest, the governor had invited President Gordon Gray, President Hollis Edens, and others to a luncheon at the governor's mansion to be held on February 9, 1955, in order to discuss the Triangle idea.[5] While this February 9 luncheon had some tangible outcomes, its historical importance is that it represented the first visible evidence that the governor was interested in the Research Triangle idea and willing to devote his energies toward taking it a step further. One outcome of the meeting was that each institution agreed, in principle, to conduct an inventory of its in-house resources (faculty as well as facilities) in an effort to better assess its ability to attract research-based companies into the area.

## THE RESEARCH TRIANGLE DEVELOPMENT COUNCIL

By April 1955, the beginnings of an organizational structure had been formed. A note from Gordon Gray to Harris Purks referred to the first meeting related to the Research Triangle as taking place in Gray's office at 2:30 P.M. on April 7.

There are no minutes from this meeting, but an important discussion item may have been the relationship between the universities and Guest's development activities. On April 4, 1955, Guest sent to Gray a report that he had prepared on the universities' resources, entitled "Research Triangle of North Carolina." Guest had planned to use this report for his own publicity. On page 1 of the report Guest wrote, "Under *prescribed policies* [emphasis added], these institutions will continue to cooperate with industrial research organizations in the prosecution of research in the public interest." This statement could easily have been viewed as rather bold and presumptuous, and it no doubt caused university officials to worry.

The Research Triangle Development Council was organized, and Governor Hodges asked Robert Hanes to serve as chairman. There is some confusion in the record as to how the council's organizational structure came about. Both Hamilton (1966) and Jones (1985), who drew on Hamilton's research, refer to a March 1955 report entitled "An Outline of the Research Triangle Organization and Its Policies," written by Malcolm Campbell, William Newell, Brandon Hodges, and Romeo Guest. However, Case (1991a) has no recollection of such a report, and Newell (1992, 1993) is certain that he did not write one or participate in discussions about one. In addition, Governor Hodges did not mention such a report when he wrote, "There was a need for organization, and, with North Carolina's future at stake, there was also a need for the maximum action. A Governor's Research Triangle Committee was formed in the spring of 1955 and the late Robert M. Hanes of Winston-Salem was named chairman" (Hodges 1962, p. 205).[6] According to Aycock (1991), Hanes was the type of individual who was interested in anything "for the good of the state."

The council's minutes showed that their first formal meeting took place in Governor Hodges's office on May 27, 1955.[7] At that meeting the members agreed on an important statement of vision:[8] "Research Triangle is an effort to make use of the triangle educational institutions . . . in the development of a research center which will attract business investment and which will give aid to North Carolina industry." It was also decided that a committee, the Research Triangle Development Committee or Working Committee, would be assembled, with Harold Lampe as chairman.[9]

On July 21, 1955, at the first meeting of the Working Committee,[10] Hanes set forth the Research Triangle Development Council's concept and mission statement, and Brandon Hodges discussed possible organizational procedures for both the council and the Working Committee. As recorded in the minutes,

[The Triangle] idea had grown out of a realization that per capita income within the state should be increased, and that the state was not getting its share of the large amount of investment being put into research and development activities. . . . *The problem for the Working Committee is to develop a program which will not endanger the purposes of each institution but which would use them as a background to develop a research area and to give to the people of North Carolina badly needed training, more employment opportunities and new products.*[11] . . . What we want to do is to place this great opportunity for formalizing a program in the hands of the Working Committee where the institutions will be absolutely protected and where your information and imagination will develop a program that we can go out and sell.

Also mentioned at this meeting was the possibility of establishing a research institute somewhere within the Triangle; this idea had been articulated earlier by Paul Gross of Duke. Following up on a previous discussion, Hanes observed to all present that "an inventory of proved competency might be a good place [for the committee] to start."

Two subcommittees within the Working Committee were established. The committee organized an Inventory Preparation Subcommittee, with Marcus Hobbs as chairman,[12] and a Program and Plans Subcommittee, with Campbell as chairman.[13] The latter group was charged with looking at various organizational possibilities for the Research Triangle.

On September 12, 1955, the Program and Plans Subcommittee distributed its report to the Working Committee. The focus of the plan was clear: the subcommittee recommended an organization, to be called the Governor's Research Triangle Council, that would "bring to the attention of industrial executives the potential of the Research Triangle to the conduct of their own research programs, and to focus this attention, given the opportunity, on specific areas of university cooperation." The subcommittee also recorded in its minutes a very clear statement about the role of the universities in the Triangle project:

The basic concept of the Research Triangle is that North Carolina possesses a unique combination of educational and research resources and communication facilities eminently suitable to the fostering of industrial research. It is not anticipated that the three universities in the Triangle shall engage directly in the conduct of industrial research, except under carefully designed and administered policies. Rather, the principal functions of the Universities are to stimulate industrial research by the research atmosphere their very existence creates, and to supplement industrial-research talents and facilities by providing a wellspring of knowledge and talents for the stimulation and guidance of research by industrial firms.

This is an important statement, and one that at the time was often overlooked and misunderstood by nonacademics. The universities saw themselves as magnets to attract research companies to the area, not as participants in the those companies' research efforts. All too often this subtle difference was ignored. It was not uncommon for others to volunteer the time and talents of the universities when speaking about the Research Triangle. For example, the *Raleigh News and Observer* reported on September 29, 1956, that Governor Hodges referred to the Research Triangle as a project designed for research laboratories and firms "*to fully utilize* [emphasis added] the research facilities of Duke University, the University of North Carolina, and N.C. State College."

There is a fine line between viewing the universities as a supporting resource and viewing them as active players in the development of the Triangle concept. This difference seemed to have eluded Guest. Harper (1991) recalled an event that Brandon Hodges told him about—a small meeting in Chapel Hill between Romeo Guest, Brandon Hodges, Governor Hodges, the two university presidents, and a small group of faculty. Guest was explaining the Research Triangle idea and how he would sell to companies the talents of the faculty. William Carmichael of the Consolidated University said, "Let me see, Romeo, if I really understand what it is we are talking about here, you want the professors here and all of us to be the prostitutes and you're going to be the pimp" (Harper 1991). Guest never really understood the implications of Carmichael's remark.[14]

The subcommittee also recommended that the position of executive secretary of the Working Committee be created to "provide a communication center for keeping all interested parties informed of all activities." At the October 20 meeting of the Working Committee, the idea of an executive secretary was again discussed, and Brandon

Hodges noted "the need of a high caliber man who has got to be a salesman and who can put himself on anyone's level."

The recommendations of Campbell's subcommittee were formally accepted at the November 7, 1955 meeting of the Research Triangle Development Council. At that meeting, Grady Rankin moved "that Mr. Hanes and Mr. Brandon Hodges, together with three others, one from each educational institution represented, comprise a committee to select an executive secretary, with power to act." This committee was formed, and it included Working Committee members Harold Lampe, Marcus Hobbs, and Henry Clark.

Also discussed at this November 7 council meeting was the idea that the Research Triangle project should be maintained as a private effort. Brandon Hodges initiated this discussion, and Governor Hodges agreed with the idea for the time being.

Marcus Hobbs (1991) believes that the people involved at this time did not have much of a vision of what was to come. They were busy faculty members, each trying to do their individual jobs on a day-to-day basis. Had they been more farsighted, they might have anticipated the inevitable conflict between a private Research Triangle venture and a university support base.

The Inventory Preparation Subcommittee, chaired by Marcus Hobbs, completed its task by December; Hanes contributed personal funds to have the subcommittee's report typed. The subcommittee distributed its "Inventory of Selected Resources of the Research Triangle" at the January 26, 1956 meeting of the Working Committee. The subcommittee members had identified, on the staff of the three institutions, approximately nine hundred individuals in fields that could eventually be related to the broadly defined mission of the Research Triangle. (It was also noted at this meeting that if there were an executive secretary, he could have summarized the 212-page report!)

At the March 18, 1956 meeting of the Working Committee, discussions continued about an executive secretary. A proposal was made that the salary for the executive secretary should be $15,000 per year, with a $5,000 budget. It was also proposed that the Research Triangle Development Council establish itself in Raleigh with an annual budget of between $35,000 and $50,000. Hanes agreed to raise funds to establish an office in Raleigh (Aycock 1991). It was decided at the May 9 meeting of the council that Hanes would contact Governor Hodges regarding his recommendations for an executive secretary to the council.[15]

Although there was not yet an executive secretary, the importance of raising money became more evident. In July 1956, Hanes met with the governor to discuss the suggestion that the council have a non-profit status so that donors could receive tax benefits. The governor agreed and, being one who disliked details, told Hanes and Brandon Hodges, "You work out something" (Aycock 1989).[16] And they did precisely that.

## THE RESEARCH TRIANGLE COMMITTEE, INC.

William C. Friday succeeded Gordon Gray as acting president of the University of North Carolina in March 1956. When Governor Hodges requested his opinion on an executive secretary for the Research Triangle Development Council, Friday recommended George Simpson, professor of sociology at Chapel Hill.[17] As Friday (1993) recalled,

> George understood these institutions. He particularly understood State and Carolina. That's his number one asset. Number two, everybody accepted him as an academic management leader because he had been identified with President Gray, and I was Gray's assistant. . . . Thirdly, he was clearly identified in the academic community as a protégé of Howard Odum. So he had all the factors going for him. Plus, from my vantage point, I knew he could relate publicly. . . . I just never had any question about it; I didn't even think about anybody else.

Although the scope of the position was ill-defined at the time, Simpson agreed to take a one-year leave of absence from the University, beginning October 1, to become director (the new title of the position) and to develop a workable plan for the Research Triangle.

Simpson (1991) recalled that after he received Friday's call, he reflected on his knowledge about the economic conditions of the region. He knew that the state was losing students and workers and that the existing industries were stagnant. He also knew that Governor Hodges "was a doer." The Research Triangle concept fit well into Simpson's general industrial slant for economic development and into his Odum-

Figure 2. *George L. Simpson, Jr., September 1956.*

influenced thinking about collaborative research. According to Simpson, he "had only a passing knowledge that something called the Research Triangle had been mentioned in the newspapers" when Friday talked with him about working as the director (Simpson 1988, p. 4); but Simpson was also "sensitized" to the challenge, for several reasons:

> The primary reason was Howard Odum, under whom I had studied and worked, and for whom I had the greatest respect and affection. . . . As he approached retirement (1954) . . . he conceived a center for the study and use of Southern resources—human, natural and social. . . . I was also sensitized by the work I was doing on the South, and that of others in Chapel Hill. By the mid-fifties there was good reason for hope for the South's economy, especially in manufacturing. . . . At the same time, things were still on a colonial, branch-plant footing. It was clear that something more fundamental was needed—a self-starting mechanism for industrial development. Research was in the air. On the one hand, I thought that the Triangle

idea might just barely be realistic; on the other hand, that it was essential. . . . I would add another influence sensitizing me to the Triangle idea. I had just finished the study of the Coker family of Hartsville and Darlington County, S.C. The Coker story was a tour de force in the local application of science and engineering to economic development. (Simpson 1988, pp. 4–5)

After accepting the position with Friday, Simpson went to meet Governor Hodges: "It was typical Hodges—short, quick, and what do you do next" (Simpson 1991). Hodges made it clear to Simpson that he would be working for Hanes. Hodges also suggested that he go to meet Hanes in Winston-Salem and take Brandon Hodges along. Later, Simpson considered what was on Hodges's mind: "Even I at that time, as naive and uninitiated as I was, could see what [the governor] was thinking, which was that here's this young academic who really doesn't look his age—I didn't in those days—with no practical experience. . . . Bob Hanes doesn't know him or anything about him" (Simpson 1991). Simpson also later realized that Brandon Hodges was invited to the meeting with Hanes to pave the way for Simpson. Hanes could be rather to the point at times:

It was probably good that Brandon was there. . . . Mr. Hanes said, "How about money?"

I said, "I think that I need $1,000 a month plus a car."

Neither one of us said anything. . . . Then Brandon said, "George, you have to understand that Mr. Hanes has to raise the money."

As I was going out the door, Mr. Hanes said, "George, you think there's something that can be done with this?"

I said, "Yes sir."

He kinda nodded and I went on out. (Simpson 1988)

Simpson learned about ten days later that he had been hired (Simpson 1988). He was paid $12,000 a year, plus a car.

Governor Hodges invited forty-five prominent business leaders to a 1:00 P.M. luncheon on September 25, 1956, to be hosted by Hanes at the Carolina Hotel in Raleigh. The invitation letter was simple and factual; this luncheon was to be of "tremendous importance to Raleigh and the area" (Aycock 1992).

At noon that day, the Research Triangle Committee, Inc. (the new name for the "Governor's Research Triangle Council" that had been recommended by the Program and Plans Subcommittee) was incorporated by its three directors—Luther Hodges, Brandon Hodges, and Robert Hanes. According to the certificate of incorporation,

> We, the undersigned, do hereby associate for the purpose of forming and organizing a non-stock, non-profit, benevolent, charitable and educational corporation. . . . The objectives and purposes for which the corporation is formed are to encourage and promote the establishment of industrial research laboratories and other facilities in North Carolina primarily in, but not limited to, that geographical area or triangle formed by the University of North Carolina at Chapel Hill, North Carolina State College of Agriculture and Engineering of the University of North Carolina at Raleigh, and Duke University at Durham. It is the intent and purpose of the corporation to promote the use of the research facilities of the three above-named institutions through cooperation between the three institutions and cooperation between the institutions and industrial research agencies, to bring to the attention of industry throughout the country the unique and undeveloped advantages of this State and thereby attract industrial research laboratories and other facilities to this State. It is the purpose through such activity not only to attract industrial research laboratories and facilities but to attract the establishment of industries and thereby to increase opportunities of citizens of this State for employment, and to increase the per capita income of the citizens of the State.

The certificate of incorporation stated that there was to be a board of directors with three members. At this noon meeting, Luther Hodges was elected by the other two incorporators as chairman of this board.

At 12:30 P.M., Hanes and George Geoghegan, head of Wachovia Bank and Trust in Raleigh, met with selected invitees to obtain pledges prior to the 1:00 P.M. luncheon.[18] The primary purpose of the meeting was not only to provide information but also to give area leaders an opportunity to invest, for the common good, in the future of North Carolina.

It was announced at the 1:00 P.M. luncheon that the Research Triangle Committee, Inc., had been formalized.[19] Most in attendance knew about the Triangle in general terms, but according to one attendee, John Alexander (1993), then president of Raleigh Tractor and Truck Company, few knew about any of the details; the single purpose of the luncheon "was just to raise money." Pledges were made for over $10,000 (Aycock 1991). According to Alexander and J. W. York (1993), then president of Cameron Village, Inc., there was great enthusiasm about the Triangle idea on the part of everyone there. As it turned out, only four or five of those at the luncheon would refrain from taking an active part in the project (Alexander 1993). When asked why there was such broad-based support, Alexander replied (partially with the benefit of hindsight) that it was just "a good idea and good for the state."

At this event, the leadership in Raleigh strongly acknowledged their confidence in the vision of both Governor Hodges and Robert Hanes. George Geoghegan had spearheaded the efforts to raise money in Raleigh. Shortly thereafter, Hodges and Hanes met with smaller groups of business leaders in Chapel Hill and Durham for fund-raising. Watts Hill was asked to lead the effort in Durham, and Collier Cobb in Chapel Hill. According to William Saunders, Raleigh and Chapel Hill always came through, but "they had one hell of a time getting money out of Durham. . . . [Durham was] getting the apple pie all the time, yet they weren't putting out. Governor Hodges complained and complained and cried on my shoulders many times about that" (Guest 1978).

The state had now played its role as organizer—a formal organizational structure had been agreed upon, and the role of the universities had been clearly articulated. It was now time for the people of North Carolina to step forward.

# CHAPTER 3

# KEEPING ON THE PATH

*Where there is no vision, the people perish.*

—PROVERBS

## GEORGE SIMPSON: A MAN OF VISION

On October 1, 1956, George Simpson assumed his responsibilities as director of the Research Triangle Committee, Inc.[1] Soon Simpson, along with his office manager and secretary, Elizabeth Aycock, moved into an office at 118 W. Edenton Street in downtown Raleigh.[2]

Governor Hodges had loaned the committee two empty rooms on the second floor of this state-owned building. Aycock (1992) remembered that she interviewed with Simpson the week before he officially became director. Before they could talk, they had to borrow two chairs from the Water Resources Board on the first floor. Their room was empty, with the exception of a telephone. However, by the end of the first week, Robert Hanes had called Alma Desk Company; two desks, eight chairs, and a telephone table—all donations—were soon delivered. Aycock bought the coffeepot with her own money.

Simpson reflected some thirty years later about his association with Aycock: "The history of her career with the Triangle shows how very fortunate I was to have her join me. She had judgement and sincerity, and she came to believe in the Triangle idea as few did in those days. She was more of a partner than a secretary" (Simpson 1988, p. 7).

In those first two months, Simpson not only developed a clear vision of where to go and how to get there—realizing that "in economic development, it's a long time from seed to harvest" (Aycock 1991)—but also set the direction for how the committee would proceed. He knew from the beginning that if North Carolina was to move forward, it would have to do so in a practical fashion. Money could eventually be raised, but only if the project had a practical use to the state (Simpson 1991):

> An obvious way to begin the Triangle was to raise a large amount of money for research activities; land or park; an Institute, etc. . . . However, it was understood that raising a lot of money would not be the first order of business. I don't know quite how I understood this. I did not ask the Governor or Mr. Hanes. I don't remember that they or anyone else told me straight out. It was not that raising money was ruled out. Rather, the situation required that, somehow, the Triangle idea take on more reality. . . . Indeed, if that reality could be established without raising big money, so much the better. But, certainly, in the North Carolina way, some pragmatic basis for raising money had first to be established. . . . There had to be some reason beyond the intellectual and logical, beyond mere hope, to raise big money. (Simpson 1988, p. 7)

Simpson (1991) recalled that he knew how the people in North Carolina thought and operated. It was never written down or explained to him; he just knew it. The Research Triangle was a good idea, and he would have the task of showing people the project's practical importance.

Money aside, there were several obstacles to be recognized right away (Simpson 1991). First, North Carolina was in the South. The state, however, did have a progressive reputation; it reacted relatively well to the Supreme Court's 1954 *Brown v. Board of Education* decision, and this fact was widely known.[3] Second, there was a tendency for large companies to maintain their research facilities at their manufacturing sites. In a trip report dated October 23, 1956, Simpson noted after his visit with the DuPont Company in Kinston, North Carolina, that they stressed "the fact that an organization as large as DuPont would not be overly impressed by the presence of professional people at any one place, since it in effect has its own university . . . [but] all other things being equal, the Triangle would prove attractive to the DuPont people."[4] And third, there was a folk wisdom that the Route 128 and Stanford Research Park were not planned; "they just happened" (Simpson 1991). Because the nation contained only these two fledgling examples of industrial growth based on university scientific research resources, there was no clear path to follow (Larrabee 1992).

Due to these obstacles and to the natural tendency of people to question any new endeavor, many people felt a "healthy skepticism"; they believed that Governor Hodges had pushed the idea of the Research Triangle too far, or just too quickly (Simpson 1991). Simpson sensed this, and he knew that he had to proceed slowly, step by step. Still, some immediate action was needed; it would accomplish nothing to "just sit and draw up plans" (Simpson 1991).[5]

Simpson's task was made easier because there were very few internal problems in the early years. According to Simpson (1991), the Triangle represented an unprecedented coming together of previously hostile forces—banks, universities, communities, political parties, and so on.[6] "The single most important aspect [leading to the successful beginning] of the Research Triangle was the generosity of mind exhibited by all elements involved" (Simpson 1991). Simpson recalled,

> I define generosity of mind, in the first instance, in the positive way—an active desire to do good. . . . [I] also apply the term generosity of mind, in the second instance, to the hundreds of times when, often at the last minute, historical mistrust was not allowed to break things off. Nobody walked or flounced off the set. Within the geographical framework of the Triangle, it is fair to say that there was no established basis for cooperation among the various elements of the Triangle. There was, indeed, a considerable history of difficulties with respect to cooperation. . . . [G]enerosity of mind is hard to measure . . . [b]ut during and after my days with the Triangle effort, I came to know a great deal about 20 or more serious efforts in other parts of the country, efforts that failed. That, I think, is the measure.
>
> No better example [of an active desire to do good] could be found than in Marcus Hobbs of Duke—open, encouraging, straightforward. Marcus was Duke's original representative on the institutional working committee. . . . [I] paid a call on Marcus very early

after signing on. We had a good talk. As I was leaving, Marcus said, "George, do you know Paul Gross?" On learning that I was fearfully ignorant, Marcus advised me pointedly to see Dr. Gross. In his easy way, Marcus told me that if Duke was to come in strong on the Triangle, Paul Gross would have to understand why. It was one of the best pieces of advice I ever got. . . . Marcus had already done his duty. . . . [P]ointing me to Gross was one form of what I am calling generosity of mind.   (Simpson 1988, pp. 1–4)

In the summer of 1956, shortly after Simpson became director, Hanes called and asked Simpson to meet him at the Washington Duke Hotel in Durham to help raise money. According to Simpson (1991), Hanes needed a body to show the people that there was someone on whom to spend their money. Hanes spoke to the Durham group about the Research Triangle idea and told them that the governor wanted about $12,000 to $15,000 from the city to help get the project moving. Simpson recalled feeling a "coolness in the air." When Hanes finished talking, there was silence. Then George Watts Hill, chairman of the board of Durham Bank and Trust Company and a prominent Durham citizen, rose to give what could well have been the prearranged Durham response: "Well, alright; we got our guard up; but it's a good thing and we'll go along; and don't no one take advantage of us." Although seemingly abrupt, this gesture represented an unprecedented display of generosity of mind—acting on trust for the common good of North Carolina.[7]

Literature was a top priority for Simpson and a necessity for the committee. In November 1956, he completed the draft of the first brochure. Having relied on a typed version of the material to show to companies during his early site visits, Simpson had an eight-page brochure printed in December (Aycock 1994).[8] This brochure is reproduced in Appendix A. It is important to the history of the Triangle not only because it was the first publicity for what was to become Research Triangle Park but also because it foretold the type of relationship that the Park would have with the universities. On the last page, Simpson wrote thoughtfully, "The Committee works solely *within the bounds and desires* [emphasis added] of the three institutions." If the relationship between the committee and the universities had been anything different—and this is what Romeo Guest never seemed to grasp—the Research Triangle would probably have been an underwhelming effort.[9]

It has been said that "if Governor Hodges was the heart, Simpson became the brain, of the Triangle" (Hamilton 1966, p. 259). Hodges's heart had already been shown through his initial efforts to formalize an organizational structure for the Triangle, and his efforts and energies would continue to be seen throughout his tenure as governor. Simpson's insight into the future direction of the Triangle was demonstrated to all in his first written communication to the committee—his "Memorandum on the Research Triangle Program for Members and Working Committee," presented on January 18, 1957. Within three pages Simpson was able "to translate the Research Triangle dream into a concrete plan" (Franco 1985, p. 249).[10] Simpson wrote,

> The basic goal of this Committee is to develop industrial laboratories in the Research Triangle, or in some other location in North Carolina. The Committee's efforts to achieve this goal fall into two main categories. In the first category are those activities involved in the direct approach of making known the resources of the Research Triangle to appropriate people in industry and government. . . . In the second category fall those activities which require more local initiative . . . as local financing of laboratories; the building of laboratory buildings for lease; the establishment of cooperative laboratories by industrial concerns already in the state; the establishment of commercial research laboratories; and the establishment of a research institute.

His direct approach emphasized not only printed material but also site visits and personal contacts: "calls on research directors, executives, etc. . . . bringing representatives of industry to the area."[11]

The report ended with a timetable of sorts: "The program for the next few months will be primarily that involved in the direct approach . . . [and by] early summer some measure of effectiveness should be available. Local initiative matters will be dealt with as time and opportunity permit."

Simpson proposed to begin by emphasizing the following research areas of concentration, "based on a common sense approach, in which an attempt had been made to take into account the quality and quantity of research resources": pharmaceuticals, chemicals, electronics, ceramics, food products, forest products, and textiles.

Implicit in his charge for local initiatives was both the need for land and the realization that the land venture would have a for-profit component: "There is the question of a research area, which might be put into motion on a risk basis. Someone might care to buy a substantial acreage of land, build a laboratory building or buildings, on the assumption that a profit would be made in the not too distant future as other laboratories come in."

Simpson's memorandum was well received at the January 18, 1957 meeting of the Research Triangle Committee and Working Committee. The minutes recorded that Hollis Edens of Duke endorsed the report and suggested that "[we] should begin in a quiet, dignified way."[12] Edens also motioned "that a committee be appointed by the President [Hanes] to study the possibilities of the establishment of a research institute." The positive vote was unanimous.

According to Simpson (1991), university cooperation was the critical element for success, more so than the institute idea. An institute was important as a diversifying strategy: "it's just like invading Europe, you invade on several different beaches." The first meeting of this institute committee took place in March.

Regarding systematic site visits to research companies, "Simpson assembled one of the most unusual teams of traveling salesmen ever seen in business offices" (Hamilton 1966, p. 259). Governor Hodges, Simpson, and business leaders assisted whenever possible, of course, but the core comprised William F. Little from the chemistry department at Chapel Hill, William D. Stevenson and John F. Lee from the School of Engineering at State College, and Kenneth E. Penrod from the Duke Medical School. Each of these individuals wrote a brochure specific to his field of expertise, and these industry-specific brochures were used to better target the information distributed to companies.

Simpson went to the respective deans and asked them for recommendations of individuals to assist with company visits. He recalled meeting William Newell when he went to visit Malcolm Campbell, dean of textiles at State College. Newell was director of the Textile Research Center at that time. "Bill told me . . . you don't need to spend too much time on the textile industry, they don't do any research. I remember what he said. He said, 'I have sat in more air-conditioned Cadillacs than you can count hearing about how bad off the textile industry is and why they can't put the money in research' " (Simpson 1991). Based on this advice, Simpson delayed focusing on textiles. It turned out to be a wise move, because most textile-related research was done by the chemical industry.

Little (1992) recalled that at the time information for the chemistry brochure was being assembled, most faculty members thought the Triangle was a great dream. The faculty in the sciences were more circumspect than those in the other disciplines. Research in the sciences had become pure after the war, and many on the science faculties wanted to distance themselves from industrial applied research. However, according to Little, they still wanted to see it all happen, although they did not want to become directly involved. It was clear to everyone that if laboratories located in the Triangle area, students would benefit in terms of employment opportunities and the science community would be enriched.

On one of Little's trips to New York, he recalled visiting Glen Nesty of Allied Chemical Company. Nesty's office was near Wall Street. When Little arrived at the top-floor office, the two men decided to go to lunch. They walked to an elevator with only an "up" button. Once on the roof of the building, they used a wooden catwalk to cross over to the next skyscraper. After entering the next building, they walked down a spiral staircase and through the kitchen to the top balcony of the Lawyers Club. Business was conducted over martinis. When lunch was over, Little was shown to an elevator, and Nesty went back to his office via the catwalk.[13]

Over two hundred companies had been personally contacted by the end of 1957. These early visits to such companies as Texaco and American Cyanamid were a learning experience, as well as an investment that would eventually pay off. The fact of the matter was that at that time, Simpson did not have much to share with these companies except a brochure and an idea. As he put it, "We were running a bluff game in a way. We didn't have anything in that early stage" (Simpson 1991).

Romeo Guest continued to pursue, on his own, certain development-related aspects of the Research Triangle. On January 17, 1957, he wrote to Governor Hodges and Robert Hanes recommending that they purchase three thousand acres of land and have it restricted for research facilities. Guest estimated that the land would cost about $1 million, and he suggested that John Motley Morehead or John Sprunt Hill would be candidates to support the venture financially (Jones 1985).

Hanes took Guest's letter to the January 18 meeting of the Research Triangle Committee and Working Committee. Guest's idea did stimulate interest, mainly because Simpson's memorandum also mentioned the need for land. The William B. Umstead State Park was suggested as one area to consider.

Simpson, acting independently of Guest, wrote to Hanes regarding land on February 26: "I am writing about the question of securing a parcel of land in the Triangle area which might be referred to as a research campus or center." Simpson went on to mention to Hanes that "the theoretical desirability of having such a parcel of land has never been in doubt" but that he had not pushed for it at the January 18 meeting because he was not yet convinced that the timing was right. Apparently Simpson now thought the timing was right: "There is great value in having something concrete, something that can be mapped and walked over, to place before people. Something tangible stimulates the imagination. The necessity of doing this has been growing on me all along. I became finally convinced last week in Indianapolis, in talking to Dr. Carney, the vice president of Eli Lilly for Research, Development, and Control . . . [and he stated that land] would be of great value, especially in putting across the [Triangle] idea to non-scientific people."

Simpson suggested to Hanes that the leaders from the three cities, along with Governor Hodges, be assembled to discuss a joint real estate venture. However, Simpson reiterated his earlier belief that "it [meaning the real estate venture] is more likely to be feasible as a private undertaking, with some profit in view." And, in fact, it did take a private venture to begin the acquisition of land.

Simpson included in his letter to Hanes a copy of a previous letter to William P. Saunders, newly appointed director of the North Carolina Department of Conservation and Development. In his letter to Saunders, Umstead Park and Reedy Creek Park were mentioned as possible sites. Attached to the Saunders letter was a copy of the January 23 reply to Simpson, through Saunders, from Thomas W. Morse, superintendent of state parks. Morse wrote that it "would be cheaper to acquire another tract of land specifically for Research Triangle purposes than to replace land and improvements now within these two state parks."[14]

## THE RESEARCH TRIANGLE INSTITUTE: AN IDEA REBORN

As mentioned above, Edens suggested at the January 18, 1957, meeting of the Research Triangle Committee and Working Committee that a committee be formed to study the possibility of an institute—an idea originally offered by Paul Gross. The record is clear that Gross voiced the importance of an institute when Duke became involved in the thinking about the Research Triangle.[15]

At the January 18 meeting, Governor Hodges appointed Brandon Hodges to chair a subcommittee to study the institute concept.[16] This Research Triangle Institute Committee first met on March 5, 1957, in Gross's office at Duke University (Hamilton 1966), although before this meeting studies of existing institutes had been made and individuals from these institutes had been contacted (Simpson 1993c). By May the committee had completed its study of the feasibility and desirability of a contract-based research institute—that is, one that would be independent of the budgets of the three institutions (Larrabee 1992).

According to Marcus Hobbs, the institute idea was needed to keep the faculty interested in the Triangle concept (Franco 1985). Aycock (1991) observed that the institute's importance was also a sign to the corporate community that the Research Triangle leaders had enough faith in the concept to first establish their own facility.

A starting point for an institute was needed. At the urging of Dean Colvard, Simpson approached Gertrude Cox, a professor of statistics at State College and founder of the Institute of Statistics at North Carolina State. According to Caldwell (1991), State College had one of the three best statistics departments in the world at that time; the others were at Iowa State University and the London School of Economics. Cox was the obvious place to start. As Simpson recalled,

> Dean Colvard of Agriculture at State pointed me to Gertrude Cox. . . . Gertrude's group was turning away a good deal of contract work. This work might well flow to the proposed Institute, if Gertrude took the lead, with some of her people. Beyond money, the statistics group at Raleigh had a good professional standing, which was a useful way to start. More, to proceed in this way demonstrated how connections might be made among the Institute and the universities. It all was a generous and fruitful suggestion from Dean Colvard, which he helped to implement.   (Simpson 1988, p. 1)

Cox agreed to incorporate her institute into the planning efforts of what would become the Research Triangle Institute.

Brandon Hodges died on December 4, 1957. His successor to the Research Triangle Committee was George Watts Hill. At Simpson's suggestion, Hanes wrote to Hill on January 10, 1958, asking him to join the committee. The committee minutes show, however, that Hill was not formally elected until the March 15 meeting. According to Simpson, "Watts' positive approach helped mightily in relations with Durham" (Simpson 1988, p. 16). Hill not only became secretary/treasurer of the committee; he also assumed Brandon Hodges's responsibility as chairman of the now formal Research Triangle Institute Committee—a fortunate circumstance for the Institute. At the urging of Carey Bostian and William Friday, John Sprunt Hill (George Watts Hill's father) donated $16,000 in February 1958 to give Gertrude Cox the resources to develop her plans for a statistical laboratory (Larrabee 1992).[17]

Developments progressed quickly under both the leadership of Watts Hill and the wisdom of Paul Gross. On December 29, 1958, the articles of incorporation for the Research Triangle Institute were filed. On January 8, 1959, the faculties at the three institutions were informed by memorandum that on January 9 it would be announced that a research institute, known as the Research Triangle Institute, had been established.[18] Gross, the driving force in planning the Institute, recalled in later years, "[The early planners felt that] the existence of the Park may be an effective way to get [research and development] people at various companies to come here, so the Institute was heavily promoted as an outstanding resource for scientists who may work in the Park. . . . [The Institute] sold itself in some ways because we had been able to give it a lot of instant credibility particularly through the establishment of an Institute advisory committee consisting of luminaries in their fields of scientific study" (Franco 1985, pp. 126–27). The faculty memorandum continued, "The Research Triangle Institute is being established as a contract research agency, to do work for industry and government. . . . It is hoped through this Institute to provide industry in North Carolina and the South with research services not now available; to encourage the use of the research in the State and regional industry; and to extend the Research Triangle's position as a research center. . . . The Research Triangle Institute will be incorporated as a non-profit organization."[19] Faculty were also told that George R. Herbert, previously the executive associate director at the Stanford Research Institute, had been selected to be the Institute's president.[20]

## THE UNIVERSITY FACULTY

For the institutions to be a useful resource in the development of the Research Triangle, it was imperative that the faculty understand the project and, as appropriate, become involved. However, according to Gross, the early efforts of the Research Triangle project "did not always sit well with some of the ivy tower types who didn't realize that many of the most crucial questions facing science often stem from applications issues" (Franco 1985, p. 143).

Simpson also realized the importance of keeping the faculty informed.[21] Simpson recalled, "I tried to give the faculty at least a basic understanding of what this whole thing was about. You have to realize that the Governor had been going around the state for some time now predicting great things for this project, but it was clear to me that the faculty needed at least some further explanation, and, in some instances at least, a lot of assurance that this project could be good for them and the universities" (Franco 1985, p. 123).

On February 5, 1957, just over three months after accepting the position of director, he addressed the Chapel Hill faculty at the Faculty Club. His speech, entitled "The Research Triangle of North Carolina," was clearly focused. His intention was twofold. First, he wanted to inform the faculty of the previous activities that had taken place (about which some of the faculty had heard or read about in one form or another) in such a way as to explain to them the importance of the Research Triangle for the state's economic development. On this point, Simpson quoted portions of his January 18, 1957, memorandum to the Research Triangle Committee and Working Committee.

Second, he wanted to emphasize to the faculty that the Research Triangle would reinforce the academic mission of the universities.[22] Simpson described the bounds of the committee's work:

> One or two things should be said concerning the condition of this organization. First, it is necessary to state that both President Gray and President Edens at the time of organization were favorable toward the [Research Triangle] idea and quite willing to participate. At the same time, knowing the hazards and knowledgeable of their own responsibilities, they were plain spoken to the effect that *they would not acquiesce in anything that was detrimental to the character and the basic educational and research programs of their institutions* [emphasis added]. This stipulation was accepted readily by all concerned.

And, about the institutions and their faculties, Simpson was characteristically direct:

> There are inherent in the formation and work of the Research Triangle Committee certain problems as regards the institutions, and certain proper reservations on the part of the faculties. . . . There is, first, the general danger involved when a university, or universities, joins in a major way with a non-institutional group, whatever the goal. There is always the chance that the university will be taken, inadvertently, into waters in which it has no business swimming . . . and that resources and energies of the individual faculty person will be diverted to applied work, at the expense of basic research. In the same way, it may be objected that the major emphasis [of the Research Triangle] is upon the natural sciences, to the neglect of the social sciences and the humanities. Even more specifically, there are problems to be solved concerning consulting arrangements, time off from teaching and so forth. All of these are quite real problems . . . [but the] Research Triangle undertaking is comparable with what the University has done in certain other areas of the state's life. . . .

The University was among those who took an early lead in the development of public education in North Carolina. . . . A variety of efforts [in public education] were involved—efforts of leadership and stimulation. The University never undertook to administer the schools. The things that the University did undertake were appropriate on the part of a university, and they are memorable elements in the University's history.

And to refocus the faculty on the primary economic development goal of the Research Triangle, and the benefits that the universities would derive, Simpson offered these summarizing remarks:

For what we are attempting here is really the stimulation of a general movement, the development of a new state of mind, among the people of the state. Our problem in North Carolina and in the South is not essentially technical; we have available to us the same scientific information as is available elsewhere; we have the same books and substantially the same facilities for training young people in science. Our problem is essentially cultural—*it is the failure of our people to grasp the use of science in industrial development, the failure to put to work what is available, the failure to begin those chain reactions of research and invention and developing which are the hallmark of mid-twentieth century life* [emphasis added]. These three institutions, located so closely together, are really a sort of improbable peak standing above the relative sahara of scientific application to industrial development. . . . I suggest, therefore, that great advantage will accrue to the University if the Triangle area develops as we hope, and becomes known as the research center of the South, and as one of the major research and scholarly concentrations in the nation.

Simpson's commitment to his vision of what the Triangle concept could mean for the state no doubt provided him with the conviction and confidence to set the direction for others to follow. Nevertheless, some faculty members were skeptical about asking the state's leaders in economic development to play a significant role in the Research Triangle project. Simpson's presence countered this skepticism and "gave assurance to the universities that one of their men was in a position to give guidance to the Philistines" (Harper 1992).

# CHAPTER 4

# PINELANDS

*Where is the man who owes nothing*
*to the land in which he lives?*
—JEAN JACQUES ROUSSEAU

## KARL ROBBINS

Having discussed the need for land at the January 18, 1957, meeting of the Research Triangle Committee, Governor Hodges attempted to identify some initial investors in North Carolina. His initial efforts were unsuccessful, so he sought recommendations from William Saunders, director of the Department of Conservation and Development.[1] Saunders suggested that the governor contact Karl Robbins in New York.

In 1930, Karl Robbins and J. Spencer Love of Burlington Mills in Burlington, North Carolina, had purchased the Pinehurst Silk Mill in Pinehurst, North Carolina. They employed Saunders as the mill manager. In later years, Robbins bought Love's interest in the mill. The mill's name was then changed to Colonial Mills, Inc., and even later to Robbins Mills, Inc. (Guest 1977). Growth in Robbins Mills under Saunders's management was phenomenal, and eventually Saunders became president. When Robbins retired to New York in the 1950s, he asked Saunders to keep him informed of possible investment opportunities in the state (Jones 1978).

Saunders also knew Guest, because in the mid-1930s he had

Figure 3. *Initial meeting of Governor Luther H. Hodges* (left) *and Karl Robbins* (right) *at the governor's mansion, April 1957.*

employed Guest for construction work at some of Robbins's plants. Through this connection Guest had the opportunity to meet Robbins. And Governor Hodges knew Robbins, because Robbins purchased products from Marshall Fields when the governor was with that company (Guest 1977).

As the governor instructed, Saunders called Robbins on March 12, 1957, and invited him to visit North Carolina to discuss an investment opportunity with the governor.[2] The next month, on April 12, Robbins met Governor Hodges, Saunders, and George Simpson for a breakfast at the governor's mansion. According to Governor Hodges, Robbins was an easy sell:[3] "You need not say anything more, Luther. I understand. It is a wonderful idea and a money-maker. I'll back you and will put up a million dollars in the project" (Hodges 1962, p. 208).

Knowing that Robbins was the sort of man who would make a decision and then expect others to fill in the details, Saunders urged Guest to go to New York and "ask Robbins to do something about going ahead" (Guest 1977).[4] Guest did travel to New York; there he simply dictated a letter to Robbins's secretary for Robbins to sign and send to the governor. The letter authorized Guest to begin to acquire options on land, in an area yet to be determined, with the goal of five thousand acres (Guest 1977). On June 6, Robbins sent Guest his first check, for $5,000, and a second check, for $25,000, was sent at the end of that month.[5]

Simpson was kept informed of these early activities. He noted in a June 13, 1957 memo to file that he had met with Guest and others on June 3. It was decided at that meeting that "all things considered it was the best attempt to buy land near [the community of] Nelson [in Durham County]; it was essential to have frontage on the Southern Railway, and entrance to Highway 70-A; and it was important to have frontage on both sides of Highway 54." These preconditions defined fairly well the area that would become the Research Triangle Park (but which Guest referred to at that time as Evergreen Farms).[6]

In a June 3, 1957 letter to Robbins, Guest related these issues and informed him that on May 22 he had hired William Maughan, a consulting forester who had been recommended by faculty at Duke University, to purchase options on the land. Maughan began working on June 3 for fifty dollars a day. Hubert Williams, a Raleigh real estate consultant, assisted Maughan on occasion; John L. Castleberry, a civil engineer from Raleigh, surveyed for Maughan. Robbins had also retained the highly visible New York architectural firm of Voorhees, Walker, Smith, Smith, and Haines to do site planning. Their initial drawings were completed in late July (Jones 1978).

In a letter dated July 18, 1957, to the law firm of Brooks, McLendon, Brim and Holderness in Greensboro, Guest noted that Robbins had agreed to the Nelson location. (Brim, a friend of Guest's, had arranged the original planning meeting with Hollis Edens of Duke in December 1954.) Guest wrote that Robbins's purpose was to "do something for North Carolina in way of industrial expansion" as well as to undertake a financial venture. He also wrote, "[The] aim of Evergreen Farms is to provide highly restricted property for the purpose of creating a park which in effect will resemble a college campus. Associated with the research park will be a separate area on which pilot plants may be built. There will be another area on which production may be carried forward in an industrial park. All areas are to be properly separated and again are to be highly restricted." In this letter, Guest also told the law firm that it had been designated by Robbins as general counsel for the project and that Guest himself was "to receive a salary of only $1 per year plus normal real estate commission on all land that is sold by us. . . . I am to have for a period of five years a stock option on an amount of stock which has not yet been agreed upon. I believe that he [Robbins] knows that I want up to 20%." Guest also noted, "The Governor and W. P. Saunders have met and have decided that they will make arrangements through proper channels for the water supply before word gets out what is going on, if possible. . . . There is actually nowhere but Durham to go for water." And finally, Guest concluded that "Mr. Robbins has a very, very large income and that dividends to him do not mean much net. Capital gain is about the only way of having a net return worthwhile."

### THE TRIANGLE TAKES SHAPE

William Maughan was a master at secrecy. By the end of July 1957, he had optioned nearly 800 acres at an average price of $161 per acre. As shown in Figure 4, the first tracts optioned were Rape (#14), Fletcher (#19), Stallings (#3), Gray (#25), and C. H. Shipp (#21).[7] The first tract purchased was the Rigsbee tract (#2)—on July 17, these 998.97 acres were purchased for $104,000.

It was noted at the June 3 meeting between Simpson, Guest, and others that it was fortunate that one tract of land as large as the Rigsbee tract existed, but that this tract should not be acquired first. The tract was held in trust by Wachovia Bank and Trust Company for the estate of nine heirs. It was thought that if this tract were acquired too soon, information about land acquisition would spread rapidly, driving up the price of the land. According to Aycock (1992), during the first part of June, Simpson received an unexpected telephone call from Peter Williams, a realtor in Raleigh, saying that the tract could be acquired if the group moved quickly. The accounting records for C. M. Guest and Sons show that Robbins sent the necessary $79,000 directly to Wachovia Bank to complete this transaction.

As the land was being optioned, an organizational structure was also being considered. On August 19, Guest went to New York to meet with Karl Robbins and with A. C. Newlin, A. M. Pullen, and Claude C. Pierce. Newlin was Robbins's New York attorney from White and Case; Pullen, of A. M. Pullen and Company, was a Greensboro accountant involved in the land acquisition; and Pierce represented the Greensboro law firm of Brooks, McLendon, Brim and Holderness. It was agreed at this meeting that all land would be acquired under the name of "Karl Robbins, trading as Pinelands Co." (Jones 1978).

Word was now beginning to spread about the Triangle effort. The governor called a special press conference on September 10, 1957, to announce plans for a research center within the Research Triangle. Robbins was not present, but Hodges read Robbins's prepared statement: "North Carolina has been good to me and I am proud to play a part in her future growth" (Hodges 1962, p. 209).

The following day, North Carolina newspapers reported on the event and referred to the four-thousand-acre park as the "Lowes Grove research park."[8] The fact of the matter was, though, that only 3,430 acres had yet been optioned or purchased.

According to the Pinelands records, 3,559 acres had been optioned or purchased by the end of 1957, with an additional 441 pending. The total cost, when all tracts were purchased, would be $700,000, of which $275,000 had already been received from Robbins. His initial agreement with the governor was to invest $1 million—$750,000 for land and $250,000 for a water line.

On September 25, the articles of incorporation for Pinelands were drafted by Brim and signed. They were filed in Raleigh on September 30. The articles authorized five hundred shares of preferred and five hundred shares of common stock, at a $100 par value. The bylaws called for an eight-member board of directors. Guest appointed only three members: Pierce, McLendon, Jr., and Leonard, all of the firm Brooks, McLendon, Brim and Holderness. At the first meeting of the board, on October 8, Guest was elected as the president and treasurer, and McLendon as the vice president and secretary.

The first meeting of stockholders was held on November 20 in the New York office of Karl Robbins, the sole stockholder (three hundred shares). Immediately after that meeting, there was a second meeting. According to the minutes, Robbins appointed himself chairman of the

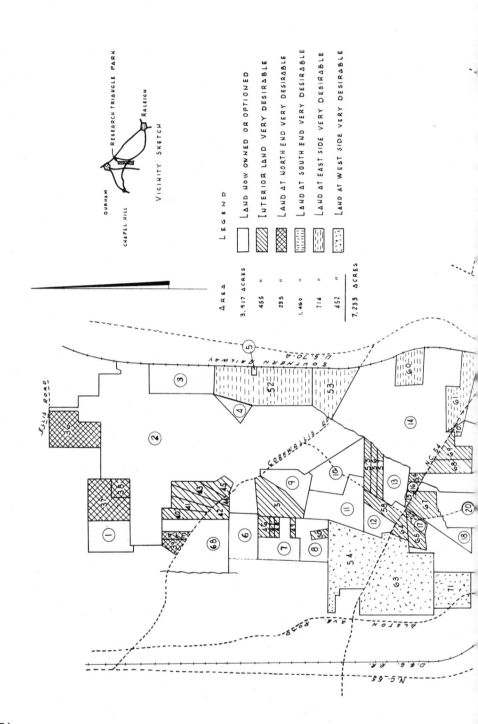

VICINITY SKETCH

RESEARCH TRIANGLE PARK

DURHAM
CHAPEL HILL
RALEIGH

LEGEND

| | | AREA |
|---|---|---|
| | LAND NOW OWNED OR OPTIONED | 3,917 ACRES |
| | INTERIOR LAND VERY DESIRABLE | 455 " |
| | LAND AT NORTH END VERY DESIRABLE | 235 " |
| | LAND AT SOUTH END VERY DESIRABLE | 1,460 " |
| | LAND AT EAST SIDE VERY DESIRABLE | 714 " |
| | LAND AT WEST SIDE VERY DESIRABLE | 452 " |
| | | 7,233 ACRES |

RESEARCH TRIANGLE PARK
OF
THE PINELANDS COMPANY, INC.
DURHAM & WAKE COUNTIES , N.C.
FEB. 10, 1958

Figure 4. Diagram of tracts within the area designated for the Research Triangle.

board, and he designated seven new directors.[9] The board met again on December 19 at Durham Bank and Trust to form an executive committee, with Robbins as chairman. This executive committee included Guest and the representatives from the three counties.

Many of the land options were due at the end of November 1957, but Pinelands had no funds to redeem them.[10] Guest went to Robbins for additional capital, but Robbins was reluctant to invest any more money in the project. According to a November 22 letter from Guest to Hill, Robbins wanted North Carolinians to own 49 percent of Pinelands, and as of then, there were no investors.

Saunders "saved the day" (Guest 1977). With the permission of Governor Hodges, Saunders made a personal loan of $100,000 to Pinelands Company.[11] The agreement called for $50,000 to be repaid to Saunders on December 1, 1958, with the remaining $50,000 to be retained by the company in favor of 250 shares of common stock (at $100 par) and a twenty-year, 5 percent debenture for $25,000. Harper (1991), who worked for Saunders at C&D at the time, speculated that Saunders was willing to invest his $100,000, against the advice of his attorneys, for several reasons: "Number one, he was a team man. He had been the governor's roommate and also teammate in baseball . . . at Chapel Hill. He was devoted to the governor. He was a cloth man if you ever saw one. In many ways [he was] a very typical textile man, but in many ways he had certain kinds of visions that were important . . . [to get] this thing going [for the good of North Carolina]."

The year ended without any options expiring, but money was a problem, and Robbins was concerned and irritated about the reluctance of North Carolinians to invest in their future. Two Pinelands Company meetings were held on December 30. According to the minutes, the first meeting was for stockholders.[12] At the meeting of the board of directors that immediately followed, the debt from the $100,000 borrowed from Saunders was formally ratified.[13] The board also agreed that the number of common shares available for sale would be increased from 500 to 7,500 and that $750,000 of 5 percent debentures would be issued. Finally, Robbins pledged that if the company could raise $265,000 from other investors, he would then contribute one dollar for every dollar invested above the $265,000, up to an additional $225,000. If this goal had been met, Robbins would have invested $500,000—one-half of his initial commitment.

## EARLY OPTIMISM

While Pinelands was busy assembling land, the members of the Research Triangle Committee continued to publicize the planned area. There were some early signs of optimism.

William Little wrote to Simpson on August 6, 1957, about his July 31 meeting with General Electric Company in Schenectady, New York. According to Little, "I feel this is the real highlight of the trip and offers the greatest promise of the companies we have so far visited."

Similarly, in an August 26 letter to Brandon Hodges, Simpson wrote, "They [American Cyanamid] came for a general look. They were not interested in details but were anxious to get the general flavor and picture of the Triangle area. I think the highlight of the visit was on Thursday night at dinner. Present were Friday and Edens and Paul Gross and about half a dozen other university people, along with Watts Hill. The conversation went along very well and they responded well." In fact, the *Raleigh Times* reported on September 11 in "Occupant Expected for Triangle" that American Cyanamid Company might be the first tenant in the "Research Triangle Park."

William Stevenson submitted a September 9 trip report to Simpson regarding his visit to IBM: "We received a favorable answer to our original letter to Mr. W. W. McDowell and he turned out to be most cordial and interested. He said he wished we had been in operation three years ago when IBM was interested in leasing or buying a laboratory site. . . . Mr. McDowell predicted success for our efforts, promised to talk about us to his associates both in and out of IBM, and even hinted that in another few years the growth of IBM would be such that they would be again interested in additional sites."

To temper this optimism, numerous trips turned out to be disappointing. For example, Little wrote to Simpson on July 25 that he had met with Dr. Voris of Hercules Powder Company in Wilmington, Delaware. Hercules was not interested in building a new lab at the time. One concern of Voris's was the quality of public schools in North Carolina. In the same letter, Little reported that he had met with Dr. Walter Ruggeberg of Atlas Powder Company. Although Ruggeberg, a Duke alumnus who had lived in Atlanta, was "sympathetic" to the South and had even visited the Park, he felt the "social climate in the South was not yet right for a move in this direction."

Even with the encouragement that the committee members and faculty received on some of their trips, 1957 was not an especially good year. There was an economic recession, and corporate research programs across the nation were curtailing their investment expenditures.[14] Brandon Hodges had died, and Robert Hanes had fallen ill. Finally, Robbins's interest in the Research Triangle had cooled. It was hoped that 1958 would prove to be a better year.

# CHAPTER 5

# DEAD ENDS, DETOURS, AND REDIRECTIONS

*Mighty things from small beginnings grow.*

—JOHN DRYDEN

## DEAD ENDS

The year 1958 began on a bright note. Pearson H. Stewart, a professional planner, was hired on January 18 as the assistant director to George Simpson (who had extended his leave from Chapel Hill). With the acreage that Pinelands had acquired, Simpson realized the need for visual material to show to prospects, and he instructed Stewart to prepare a map of the area. Figure 5 shows this first map of the Research Triangle Park of the Pinelands Company, Inc. However, many dead ends would soon be encountered.

In a January 8, 1958 letter from Governor Hodges to Karl Robbins, the governor expressed concern over Robbins's reluctance to honor his initial financial commitment to the Research Triangle:

> I am very much disturbed and concerned about recent developments in the financing of the Research Park. It is my understanding that you wouldn't put any more money in, beyond the $275,000 that you have now invested, until and unless local people match this. . . .
> It is not that we do not deeply appreciate what you have done nor that we feel that you are putting in too little money, but we could

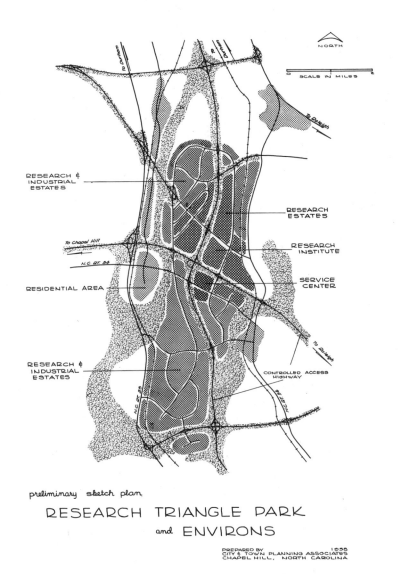

RESEARCH & INDUSTRIAL ESTATES

RESEARCH ESTATES

RESEARCH INSTITUTE

SERVICE CENTER

RESIDENTIAL AREA

RESEARCH & INDUSTRIAL ESTATES

CONTROLLED ACCESS HIGHWAY

To Durham

To Durham

To Raleigh

To Chapel Hill

N.C. RT. 54

N.C. RT. 55

N.C. RT. 55

NORTH

SCALE IN MILES

To Raleigh

*preliminary sketch plan*

RESEARCH TRIANGLE PARK
*and* ENVIRONS

PREPARED BY                                         1958
CITY & TOWN PLANNING ASSOCIATES
CHAPEL HILL, NORTH CAROLINA

Figure 5. *First planning map of the Park area. Courtesy of Robert N. Anderson, Jr. City Planning & Architects Associates.*

be tremendously embarrassed and chagrined because of the public announcement of the fact that you alone were doing it. . . . As you know, I have great affection and admiration for you and I do not want to see any misunderstandings or difficulties arise.

There has been much speculation regarding Robbins's coolness to the Triangle project. Edward Rankin, Governor Hodges's private and personal secretary, told Harper (1992) that it was Robbins's lawyer who came to the governor to explain that Robbins would not invest additional funds in Pinelands. It was also Robbins's lawyer, more so than Robbins, who was concerned about the lack of North Carolina investors. Aycock's impression was that the real concern rested with the son, Alan Robbins, who did not expect the investment ever to become profitable (Aycock 1992). Perhaps Simpson had the greatest insight into Robbins's new requirements: "Robbins came to require that North Carolina interests put up money for the Park, along with him. He came to feel vulnerable, otherwise. I caught several glints of the reason. Hodges said that Robbins had not realized as much net from the mill sale as he had thought. Robbins's family and New York lawyer thought he was unwise. Jewish leaders, I heard, chided Robbins for investing in North Carolina rather than Israel" (Simpson 1988, p. 13).

In addition to Robbins's concern about the lack of North Carolina investors—although Guest and A. A. Vanore did invest their personal funds in February[1]—Robbins was also becoming irritated with the City of Durham's delay in responding to the Pinelands Company's request for water.

All of the early planners had recognized from the beginning that water would be a problem and that Durham was the only available water source. On January 30, Watts Hill received an "assurance" from the Durham City Council that the city would cooperate with Pinelands (Jones 1978), but he was unsuccessful in obtaining a blank check for an emergency eight-inch line if a tenant was quickly found.[2] Robbins finally visited with Durham mayor E. J. Evans and the Durham City Council on February 25 and 26, respectively. He was able to obtain a promise of two thousand gallons of water per day, with the possibility of an additional thousand gallons per day if needed (Hamilton 1966; Jones 1978).[3]

In retrospect, Simpson (1991) does not recall the water problem with Durham as being "that big of a deal"; he knew that such matters take time. Stewart (1993) is also sympathetic to Durham's reluctance to build a water line. The city manager of Durham at that time was Bob Flack. According to Stewart, Flack did not believe that the Triangle idea would ever develop and saw no reason for the city to invest in such a venture. Triangle planners also had to deal with the question of sewage treatment. Durham's treatment plant was on the north side of the city, and it would not be practical to treat the Triangle's waste there. In fact, Chemstrand Corporation, the first park tenant, had to build its own package plant.

Other dead ends were also reached in early 1958. Although over two hundred industrial and governmental research organizations had been visited by committee members and faculty representatives, and hundreds of brochures had been mailed by the committee as well as by Guest, no company had yet located in the Triangle. Astra, Inc., a Milford, Connecticut company specializing in atomic energy research, had expressed an interest in the area. Through Hill's diligent efforts, a $50,000 line of credit was arranged for the company, and they did relocate—but to Raleigh rather than to the Park area.[4]

While there was general agreement among the directors of the Pinelands Company that land would eventually be given for a research institute, Robbins wanted to see first that money for an institute was being raised (Simpson 1991).[5] But no money had been raised. Such an institute, however, could act as a magnet to attract research companies to the Triangle. To those involved, this circle must have seemed endless; as Simpson put it, "The issue became like this. Robbins wanted the Institute money raised first before he deeded land, and took the final plunge into the Park (beyond options for land). On the other hand, the Governor, Hanes, etc. and I would or could not raise money for the Institute until Robbins acted. It became a difficult stalemate" (Simpson 1988, p. 13).

DETOURS

In early January 1958, the governor knew that the Research Triangle Committee had to redirect its thinking. It was becoming clear to

Figure 6. *Early planning meeting in Durham, February 1958. Karl Robbins* (second from left), *Governor Luther H. Hodges* (fourth from left), *Robert M. Hanes* (fifth from left), *George L. Simpson, Jr.* (seventh from left), *William P. Saunders* (eighth from left), *and Willard F. Babcock* (ninth from left).

all concerned that they could not rely solely on Robbins for the financial capital needed to assemble the land and see the project through. The committee would have to depart from the original plan of attracting an outside investor and try to sell stock on its own.

However, the group had little success,[6] and within a month or two the company had to borrow $250,000 to redeem more options on land.[7] And before long Pinelands needed another $35,000 to complete its business for the month of May. With help from Hill, who made a personal visit to see Robbins in New York, Robbins did advance the company an additional $55,000. Still, it was clear to all concerned that the venture could not continue on a week-to-week basis.

There was a special meeting of the board of directors of Pinelands Company on June 11 at the Pines Restaurant in Chapel Hill to consider the possibility that Dr. D. A. Goodkind from New York might

Figure 7. *Early planning meeting in Durham, February 1958.* Left to right: *Pearson H. Stewart; unidentified Durham city official; George L. Simpson, Jr.; Romeo H. Guest, Jr.; George Watts Hill.*

invest in Pinelands. Guest (1978) recalled the meeting. It was clear to all that Goodkind was interested because Pinelands was a good deal; "he wasn't coming in to be a good friend to North Carolina." According to Guest, Hill simply laid down his pen at this meeting and did not take notes. The issue of allowing Goodkind to invest was never voted upon; rather, the board delayed its decision until Goodkind was no longer interested.

By the end of June, with the $250,000 bank loan, the additional $55,000 from Robbins, and the money raised from the sale of stock, Guest was able to purchase most of the land optioned in 1957. Pinelands now owned 3,921 acres (Jones 1978).[8]

Aycock (1991) recalled Simpson's mood during this stressful summer of 1958. Simpson had vision, perhaps more than anyone else involved at that time. He knew that the Research Triangle would be a long-run venture. Aycock recalled, "One afternoon they were sand-

Figure 8. *Early planning meeting, February 1958.* Second from left to right: *Pearson H. Stewart; Governor Luther H. Hodges; Lennox Baker; Hollis Edens; George L. Simpson, Jr.*

blasting the First Baptist Church on the opposite corner from us [in downtown Raleigh], and we were looking at that. And I said, 'George, how long do you think it would take [the Park] to reach . . . a population of 50,000 or 60,000?' And he said, 'Fifty years; a hundred years.'" And after thirty-five years, there are 34,000 people employed in the Park. Simpson might just have been right!

## REDIRECTIONS

Having discussed the financial situation of Pinelands with Robert Hanes, Governor Hodges and Hanes decided that it would be best to centralize energies and ask one person to undertake the task of selling stock in Pinelands. Hanes suggested Archie Davis for the job.

In August 1958, Hanes was vacationing in Morehead City, North Carolina; Hodges was in Raleigh; and Davis was with his family at Pawleys Island, South Carolina. Hanes called Davis and asked him to

Figure 9. *Archie K. Davis.*

come to Morehead City to meet with him and the governor. No agenda was discussed over the telephone (Davis 1992).

Their request of Davis was simple—please sell stock in the Pinelands Company; the Research Triangle has the potential to be very important for the future economic direction of the state. Davis knew nothing of the Research Triangle or Pinelands Company before that meeting, but his first impression was that their concept was flawed: "To me, I just felt without knowing anything about it, it just didn't make sense. If this indeed was designed for public service, then it would be much easier to raise money from corporations and institutions and the like, who were interested in serving the State of North Carolina, by making a contribution" (Davis 1992). Without hesitation, Davis agreed not to sell stock but rather to solicit contributions.

While he saw the public service merits of the idea, he also agreed to the undertaking because of who was asking: "That's when I made up my mind . . . because there was no man whom I admired more than Bob Hanes. I was devoted to him. He started me off with the bank. There's no man whom I've ever observed with whom I got a greater sense of determination to honor his confidence in me" (Davis 1992).

According to Davis (1992), Governor Hodges immediately "jumped on the contribution notion," but Hanes did not see it right away. Hanes's view was that a venture with this much risk should be tied to profit.[9] He later changed his mind.

In later years, Davis reflected on the nonprofit nature of his agreement to raise money: "It had become clear to me that the entire effort had taken a wrong direction, and needed a new approach. Part of the problem was that some of the people involved in Pinelands didn't have a very good sense of what higher education would support, and were reluctant to make any changes that would threaten their right to make money on the project" (Franco 1985, p. 104).

On September 8, 1958, Governor Hodges met with Davis, Gross, Simpson, and others, at the governor's mansion to discuss in detail the goals of the campaign. They knew that Pinelands would eventually have to be liquidated. The company had borrowed $250,000 from various banks and $100,000 from Saunders. In addition, there was approximately $65,000 in stocks and notes issued to various individuals. The company's total debt thus came to $415,000. Simpson had estimated that the Institute would need $500,000 to finance its operations until it could assemble enough staff and attract sufficient contracts to become self-supporting (Herbert 1994). Paul Gross led the discussion about the Institute at this meeting. It was his belief that the Institute could not be controlled by the committee; it must be controlled instead by the three universities. Simpson recalled later that Gross told him that the $500,000 for the Institute would be a precondition for Duke's involvement (Larrabee 1992).

Davis rounded the total of these amounts to $1 million and added to it $250,000 for a main building. A total of $1.25 million would thus be needed.[10]

The annual meeting of the members of the Research Triangle Committee was held on October 22 at the governor's mansion. Prior to this meeting, Davis had gone to New York to meet with Robbins to resolve a matter that had to be settled before the committee could proceed: he and Robbins talked at an outdoor cafe on Fifty-ninth Street, and Robbins agreed that all of the Pinelands stock would be turned over to the committee when the money was raised. Davis followed up his visit with a letter dated October 9, 1958. This letter set forth that all stockholders in Pinelands would take a three-year note, plus interest, for their shares.

At the October 22 meeting, Davis presented his nonprofit program and goals; "Archie was like a bucket of water to people who were pretty thirsty" (Simpson 1991). According to the minutes, "Davis noted that both the Research Institute and the Research Park have a very definite public character and that, consequently, each should be nonprofit." He suggested that the Park be organized in such a way that any funds remaining after development and property acquisition costs could go to the Research Institute, or to the committee for the benefit of the Institute. Then, any funds remaining in the Institute after operating costs could go to the three Triangle universities for basic research activities. The committee voted unanimously to approve Davis's plan, contingent on his effort to raise $1,000,000 for the committee and $250,000 for a main building.

At this meeting the Research Institute Committee also recommended hiring George Herbert as president, at an annual salary of $25,000, plus a house and a country club membership for professional use. Governor Hodges endorsed this recommendation, and Herbert was hired effective December 1, 1958.

Davis began the fund-raising campaign in his home town of Winston-Salem. It was critical to Davis that he begin with prior commitments. Over $450,000 was pledged by Winston-Salem businesses. Davis (1992) recalled the commitment from Winston-Salem when, as discussed in Chapter 8, the City of Durham tried to annex the Park: "Down the road I had to tell them down in Durham when they were thinking about taking this place over, I said, 'don't forget if it hadn't been for the people in Winston-Salem, [there] wouldn't be a Park down here.'"

Davis (1992) is proud of the fact that no one ever turned down a request for money. When I asked why he was so successful, he replied, "Because I was doing it in the name of Bob Hanes and the governor." Davis also noted that among these donors there was more than a "generosity of spirit"; there was also a "dedication to the State of North Carolina."

As often happens to the best-laid plans, the scheme to liquidate Pinelands ran into a snag: Robbins changed his mind. During the financial campaign, Davis received word that Robbins was no longer willing to sell his shares in Pinelands. Davis was in Greensboro at the time and remembered calling Robbins from a pay telephone for clarification of this rumor. He told Robbins that he had already raised $700,000 and was on his way to Asheville to ask for an additional $50,000 from a prospect company. Davis thought that he had settled the issue, but he called Robbins again from Asheville just to be sure that he would turn in his stock. Robbins agreed, and according to Davis (1992), "I kept on."

Davis raised the entire $1.25 million through one-on-one conversations.[11] He traveled the state, at his own expense, speaking primarily with Hanes's friends and others of that generation. Simpson recalled, "I remembered that [Davis] carried an envelope in his inside coat pocket, with the list of possible donors on it. It was a great tribute to Davis, to Mr. Hanes, to the governor, to Watts Hill, and to the 'establishment' donors that the initial money was raised, on faith and in good humor" (Simpson 1988, p. 15).

Of particular emphasis, when Davis met with business leaders, was the Institute. The business leaders of the state could relate very well to the importance of an Institute for the common good of the universities and the Park. According to Friday (1993), people were giving to the Park to help the universities. In those days there was "tremendous university loyalty in the corporate leadership structure."

Davis had made a personal commitment to raise the $1.25 million by December 31, 1958. A few days before Christmas, Davis was only $100,000 short of this goal. John Motley Morehead was visiting the governor and staying at the governor's mansion. Hodges asked Davis to come and ask Morehead for the $100,000. The governor himself was understandably reluctant to ask, because Morehead was his guest. Davis (1992) agreed:

> And then when it came to the point [in the conversation] that I had to really talk to Mr. Morehead, the governor absented himself. And I took Mr. Morehead, and I'll never forget, into the dining room. We were looking out the window, and I told him our problem that we needed $100,000. . . . We were right at the very . . . end of this thing and we needed $100,000. . . . He looked out of the window, he thought and didn't say anything. . . . He looked at me and finally he

said, "This is what I can do. I will give you $33,333.33 on January 1 of next year [one day past the goal date]. . . . It will be your responsibility to call me on January 1 a year from now, and if I am living I will give you $33,333.33. And then the year after that, if I am living and you call me, I'll give you $33,333.33." It was on the strength of that, that Luther and I agreed that if anything happened to him during that two-year span, that he and I, some way or another, would guarantee to make whatever was left good. . . . So it was on the strength of that, that we felt we could honorably go ahead with the deal and not go back and say we didn't raise the money.

For the record, Morehead did contribute $99,999.99 in the time prescribed. And the other $0.01 was carried on the books for several years (Aycock 1992).

The liquidation of the Pinelands Company could now begin.[12]

# CHAPTER 6

# A NEW BEGINNING

*'Tis well an old age is out,*
*And time to begin a new.*
—JOHN DRYDEN

## JANUARY 9, 1959

An event that took place on January 9, 1959, "was one of the most significant events in the history of North Carolina" (Hodges 1962, p. 213): a luncheon was held in the Virginia Dare Ballroom at the Sir Walter Hotel in Raleigh. There Governor Hodges announced to some 600 of the leading businesspeople in the state that Archie Davis had raised $1.425 million. Many of the more than 850 donors had given more than they had originally pledged, and Robert Hanes's family and many of his friends had increased their pledges in order to have the main building named in his honor (Aycock 1991).[1]

It was also announced that these funds would be used for three purposes: to establish the Research Triangle Institute to do contract research for business, industry, and government;[2] to construct a new building to house the Institute in the research park in the center of the Research Triangle area; and to acquire the land assembled by Karl Robbins and pass control of his venture to the nonprofit Research Triangle Foundation.

The Research Triangle Institute would be housed in a new building to be called the Hanes Building. The announcement of the naming of this building came as a surprise to Robert Hanes, who had fallen ill the previous year. Elizabeth Aycock (1992) recalled that Hanes, who was seated at the head table, accepted this honor and said that he was pleased that it came in the "late afternoon or early evening of my life."[3]

On December 29, 1958, the Research Triangle Institute had been incorporated as a nonprofit organization. The minutes show that at 10:00 A.M. on the morning of January 9, 1959, the members of the Research Triangle Institute board met for the first time and elected George Watts Hill as chairman, George Herbert as president, Orene K. Gibson as secretary, Walter Sledge as treasurer, and M. Cecil Ernst as assistant treasurer. Then, at 11:15 A.M., the board met again to elect the Institute's twenty-five governors.[4]

The minutes of the Research Triangle Committee showed that earlier there had been a special meeting of its members on January 2, 1959, in Edens's office at Duke University. Friday and Hill were present, but not Hanes. At this meeting, a December 28, 1958 amendment to the Research Triangle Committee's charter, changing its name to the Research Triangle Foundation of North Carolina, was formally approved. Also, new bylaws were discussed that would increase the number of directors to twenty-five.[5] Then, at 10:30 A.M. on the morning of January 9, the directors of the Foundation met and elected Hanes as chairman of the board,[6] Archie K. Davis as president,[7] G. Akers Moore, Jr., as vice president, George Watts Hill as secretary, Thomas W. Alexander as treasurer, and Elizabeth J. Aycock as assistant secretary/treasurer.[8] Simpson remained as director of the Foundation and Stewart as the associate director. At this 10:30 A.M. meeting, all of the sale agreements with Pinelands Company were signed. The newly organized Pinelands would operate as a subsidiary of the Foundation, and it would move its office from Greensboro to Raleigh.[9]

Guest resigned as president of Pinelands on January 13, 1959. At the May 11, 1959 meeting of the directors of the Foundation, Hill read Guest's May 8 letter of resignation. The minutes state that Guest "was one of the originators of the Research Triangle Program." Hugh Chatham was appointed to take Guest's place on the board. The minutes also show that Hill was asked to express to Guest the board's regret.

Figure 10. *Officers and directors of the Pinelands Company, late 1959.* Top left to right: *James C. Little; Clyde A. Dillon; John M. Dozier; Worth A. Lutz; George P. Geoghegan, Jr.; Ralph C. Price.* Bottom left to right: *Pearson H. Stewart; Thomas W. Alexander; G. Akers Moore, Jr.; Elizabeth Aycock; James B. Shea, Jr.*

On November 17, 1959, after Guest had resigned, Governor Hodges wrote to him: "May I thank you for what you have done and I again say to you as I have said to many, many other people that you are really the person that gave birth to the idea of the Research Triangle." This was an important letter in Guest's mind, one that he referred to often in his later years when interviewed about the Triangle.[10]

As one scholar observed nearly a decade later, "So was built into the corporate structure of the Triangle the remarkable collaboration of state, business, and higher education that had created it" (Hamilton 1966, p. 268). Extremely able individuals had come forward in a generally unselfish manner for the good of the state.

On January 9, one story ended and another began. Myriad ideas had finally come together to form the Research Triangle Institute and the Research Triangle Foundation. What followed is perhaps the greatest success story in the history of economic development efforts.

The interplay of unique events and talented individuals had culminated with the announcement of January 9. Against the backdrop of these events was Simpson's matter-of-fact final report to the committee—a document dated January 8 and titled "The Research Triangle Committee—A Final Report of Activities," in which he summarized the successes of the past year:

1. a continued information program;
2. ECSCO, an engineering firm specializing in test facilities and ground support equipment for missiles and aircraft, announced their plans to open an East Coast office and to build a research facility in the Park;
3. the establishment of a research institute;
4. the preparation of preliminary site plans for a park; and
5. the preparation of the preliminary form of a regional planning authority bill.[11]

Although 1958 started out with several activities and plans that led to dead ends, the year ended with a number of accomplishments. And these accomplishments were realized without one cent of state funding! Moreover, the participating universities did not make any direct investments in the undertaking.

But what about the future? Probably only a very few of those present on the afternoon of January 9 had a complete vision of what is today Research Triangle Park. Simpson was one who did, however. Shortly after the luncheon he wrote,[12] "Indeed, because North Carolina had no special advantage or resource in the area of economic development, it will be the intangible qualities of the State that will determine the course of development over the next fifteen years." And North Carolina had the intangibles not only to ride the storms that developed over the next few years but also to keep these short-term obstacles within the perspective of the Triangle's long-term potential.

# CHAPTER 7

# SLOWLY MOVING FORWARD

*Thus progress itself increases the urgency of the warning*
*that in the economic world . . . progress must be slow.*
— ALFRED MARSHALL

## PREPARING TO REORGANIZE AGAIN

Although the Foundation owned all of the Pinelands stock, Pinelands was still responsible for capital gains taxes on any land that it sold. The only potential way to avoid this tax obligation was to liquidate Pinelands into the nonprofit Foundation. To be sure that such a move would not be viewed as tax avoidance, the Foundation's officers had to consult the Internal Revenue Service.

Archie Davis (1992) recalled going to visit the head of the Greensboro IRS for a preliminary ruling on this matter. All Davis was told was that "it would be worth a try." He was advised that if he wanted to be absolutely sure, he should take the issue to Washington, but that if the ruling there were negative, then "school was out."

Based on the guarded recommendation from the Greensboro office, the Foundation planned to liquidate Pinelands when that move became financially possible.[1] The liquidation finally occurred on August 31, 1965, although final approval for the transfer of property was not received from the IRS until 1968.

What turned out to be critical in the IRS decision was the fact that the original 1956 articles of incorporation for the Research Triangle

Committee stated that "Upon the dissolution of this corporation, all assets of the corporation shall be divided equally among the University of North Carolina at Chapel Hill, North Carolina State College of Agriculture and Engineering of the University of North Carolina at Raleigh, and Duke University at Durham, to be used by such institutions for the purposes for which said institutions were founded." Because the name of the committee was changed by charter amendment, this dissolution stipulation still applied to the Foundation and to all of the assets that it would own after the liquidation of Pinelands.

The year-end audited statements of the Foundation show that it began to distribute moneys to the universities in 1968. A cash grant of $10,000 was given to each institution in 1968, in 1970, and in 1972. The monies were used for graduate fellowships.

## CHEMSTRAND CORPORATION

In the mid-1950s, Chemstrand Corporation, then jointly owned by Monsanto Corporation and American Viscose, contracted with Booz, Allen and Hamilton, a Boston consulting firm, for an evaluation of potential locations for a new chemical fiber research facility. Booz, Allen identified twenty-one sites (of which the Triangle was not one) and recommended that Chemstrand relocate from Decatur, Alabama, to Princeton, New Jersey.

As early as 1957, George Simpson had been in contact with Chemstrand representatives about the Research Triangle area (Aycock 1992). Apparently, the Triangle was not a highly regarded location by the Booz, Allen consultants. However, William Little (1992), one of the early university representatives to travel to companies selling the Research Triangle idea, had the opportunity to meet Chemstrand's Bruce Ballentine in the spring of 1958, when Ballentine was on the Chapel Hill campus recruiting new Ph.D. chemists. Little showed him brochures, and "his reaction was great." Although there were a number of Chapel Hill and State College graduates working for Chemstrand, Ballentine was not encouraging to Little; he emphasized that Chemstrand had already decided to move to Princeton.[2] But he agreed to take the materials back to Decatur and show them to David W. Chaney, their vice president for research.

Efforts to attract Chemstrand did not stop here. A faculty delegation representing all three of the universities went to Decatur to meet with the Chemstrand officials. Chaney recalled,

> We were all impressed in two ways. First it was assuring to see that the faculty of the three schools were integral to the entire effort and even willing to come down to Alabama to meet with us. Secondly, in some of the other areas that we were considering, we had to take all the initiative in setting up meetings, getting to see the right people and things like that. With the North Carolina people, you just got a really good feeling that they wanted to work with you and help you succeed.   (Franco 1985, p. 133)

It did not take Chaney and Chemstrand long to decide in favor of the Research Triangle. Chaney visited the area and met with both Pearson Stewart and representatives from State College. By this time George Simpson had returned to his position as professor at the University of North Carolina at Chapel Hill, although he remained heavily involved with the Institute.[3]

In late May, Carl O. Hoyer, Chemstrand's vice president and general manager of manufacturing, engineering, and development, came to Raleigh to meet with the governor to inform him about Chemstrand's decision to locate in the Triangle.[4] The *Winston-Salem Journal-Sentinel*, among other newspapers, reported this development on May 26, 1959, in an article titled "State's Research Triangle Gets First Big Customer: Chemstrand to Build Lab."[5]

Chemstrand purchased one hundred acres of land from the new Pinelands Company.[6] They closed on the land in the first few days of October 1959 and started construction on October 5. The Chemstrand building was dedicated on February 1, 1961.[7] The newspapers reported that Luther Hodges (then U.S. Secretary of Commerce) and Governor Terry Sanford attended the dedication ceremony. Paul Gross of Duke gave the dedication address.

Two important factors brought about Chemstrand's change in plans, according to Chaney. One was the proximity of the three major universities, and the other was the overall quality of life, including the area's cosmopolitan citizenry, the cultural advantages that the three cities offered, the climate, and the cost of living (Franco 1985).

The relationship between Chemstrand and the universities proved beneficial to all concerned. Chemstrand's scientists frequently taught courses at State College and Chapel Hill, and State's faculty were continuously engaged in the company's various research projects. In fact, according to Chaney, "The more I got involved in higher education through my work with Chemstrand, the more I began to understand its importance" (Franco 1985, p. 179). In fact, after leaving Chemstrand, Chaney became dean of State's School of Textiles.

The quickness with which Chemstrand decided to locate in the Triangle and construct a facility fast-forwarded other critical planning issues. Covenants and restrictions had to be finalized, and they had to meet with Chemstrand's approval. In addition, the continuing issue of water from the City of Durham had to be resolved.

## PLANNING THE PARK

Stewart was an exceptional professional planner. Much of the groundwork for planning the Park had already been completed, but when Chemstrand announced its intention to move into the Park on such short notice, Stewart certainly demonstrated his abilities.

At the March 14, 1959 meeting of the new Pinelands Company, some general development policies for the Park had been adopted.[8] These policies mandated "that eligible occupants of the Research Triangle Park be design, research and related operations . . . or in more general terms, uses that require a high degree of scientific input and which can benefit from a locational relationship with the academic community." Anticipated occupants were identified to be research laboratories, basic and applied; prototype product plants; pilot plants; and custom or specification production plants.

Regarding covenants and restrictions, at this meeting the board approved a design review board with the basic authority over building and site design in the Park. All parking was to be off-street; the maximum building average of the sites was to be in the 5 percent to 30 percent range, with 5 percent to 10 percent as a basis for the overall Park; six acres was the minimum acreage per tenant; and "no odors, noise, radiation, vibration, fumes, dust, gases, smoke, etc., [were] to be permitted to cross property lines."

It was never intended that there be manufacturing in the Park. The original document of Covenants and Restrictions of September 1, 1959, stated, "No manufacturing or processing enterprises shall be conducted except as such activities are adjuncts of research activities conducted within the Research Triangle Park. There shall be no goods or products manufactured primarily for sale." Stewart (1993) recalled that there was a lot of anguish about this point within the committee. Both sides of the issue were openly debated. Simpson was in favor of manufacturing. When Governor Hodges asked what he thought, he simply reminded the governor that everyone on Route 128 makes something, and "that did it" (Stewart 1993).

Zoning provisions were approved on January 4, 1960: "Not more than five (5) percent of the total area of a tract shall be covered by buildings and the total floor area of all buildings shall not exceed an area equal to ten (10) percent of the total area of a tract." But on August 5, 1963, a zoning change was approved, because a potential tenant was lost as a result of the 5 percent limitation: "Not more than fifteen (15) percent of the total area of a tract shall be covered by buildings."

In early April, state representative Watts Hill, Jr., son of Durham's George Watts Hill, introduced into the state legislature a bill to create a Research Triangle Regional Planning Commission. Its function would be to assure an orderly development of the Park. The General Assembly approved the commission the following month.[9]

Along with covenants and restrictions, roads were critical to the planning of the Park. There were only two paved roads in the area at that time—Cornwallis Road and Highway 54.[10] While the state, as intended, had refrained from contributing any money to the project thus far, on June 24, 1959, Governor Hodges did allocate $150,000 for a new road to connect Highway 54 and Cornwallis in order to provide access within the Park.

At the March 14, 1959 meeting of Pinelands, a motion was made to request that the state build such a road. Willard F. Babcock was the state highway administrator at this time. He and Stewart met frequently, because the road could not be started until the planning was completed, and the planning could not be completed until the planners knew where the road would be. In addition to assisting the development of the Park with a new road, in 1963 the North Carolina

State Highway Commission, with the cooperation of the U.S. Bureau of Public Roads, purchased 102 acres of land from the Foundation for the right-of-way for this road, at a price of $65,000. The minutes of the Foundation from November 13, 1963, refer to this proposed road as the Research Triangle Freeway. It took an additional three years to complete. This road eventually became part of what is now Interstate 40.

Finally, there was the issue of water. In late February 1958, the City of Durham had promised the committee two thousand gallons of water per day, with the possibility of one thousand more gallons per day, if needed. At the February 2, 1959 meeting of the executive committees of the Foundation and of Pinelands, Davis announced that the city was now requiring the Park to build the water line as well, at an estimated cost of $400,000.[11] According to common practice, the city charged all of its customers outside of the city limits twice its normal rate for water, and no exception would be made for the Park.

Davis (1992) remembers quite clearly his irritation at having to pay for the water line *and* having to pay double for water: "That got under my skin, they were really costing us." In later years Davis felt that the Park had sufficiently increased Durham's tax base and that the least they could do was return the $400,000, but the city refused: "I could not get any satisfaction." Finally he told the city that he would go public and start litigation matters if the Park's $400,000 was not paid back. In March 1974, the Park's water line was sold to the City of Durham for $400,000.

## PROGRESS COMES SLOWLY

Indeed, the early part of 1959 was an exciting time. Chemstrand was on board, and there was a commitment from ECSCO to locate in the Park.[12] However, the early momentum slowed quickly. The ten acres that ECSCO had reserved in the Park were never purchased.

It is reasonable that the Park's leaders felt some disappointment about the immediate slowness of activity. Governor Hodges wrote to Davis, "I confess I am confused and disturbed as I know you must be" (Hamilton 1966, p. 273). James B. Shea, Jr., was hired in February 1959, in an effort to help promote the Park.[13]

Money was needed that summer. An option on Tract #52, for

191.08 acres, would expire on August 1, 1959, and the Park did not have the money to purchase the land. Because this tract was important to the overall development of the Park,[14] Hill advised Moore that for the good of the Park, he would purchase the land through Durham Realty and Insurance Company and hold it until the Park had sufficient funds. The Pinelands minutes on August 6, 1959, stated,

> Be it resolved by the Board of Directors of Pinelands Company, Incorporated that it does express its sincere appreciation to Mr. George Watts Hill for his purchase of Tract No. 52 in the Research Triangle Park; that by purchasing said tract and holding it for future conveyance to this corporation, *without hope or expectation of personal gain* [emphasis added], Mr. Hill has again demonstrated by his actions his dedication to the concept of a truly great research center developed for the common good of the citizenry of North Carolina.

Pinelands purchased the tract from Durham Realty on March 14, 1961, for $87,644.93.

In January 1960, Karl Robbins died. At the May 11, 1960 meeting of the Foundation's board of directors, the following resolution was read: "Now be it therefore resolved that the Research Triangle Foundation of North Carolina, the Research Triangle Park, and the Research Triangle Institute are deeply grateful for [the actions] of Karl Robbins, a gratitude shared by the people of North Carolina, and these three organizations pledge their full efforts to the completion of the task which Mr. Robbins so well helped to begin."

The Sale of Pinelands Agreement of December 3, 1958, called for stockholders to be paid by December 3, 1961, but Robbins's untimely death put pressure on the Foundation to settle its debt with his estate. At the November 30, 1960 meeting of the Foundation, Davis reviewed the outstanding obligations that were due on December 3, 1961: 5,051 shares of stock to be redeemed for $117.50 (or $593,492.50) and a $250,000 mortgage with Wachovia Bank. Davis suggested that the Foundation borrow approximately $1.3 million for these obligations; purchase miscellaneous tracts of land, in order to bring the total acreage of the Park to nearly five thousand; and continue to operate the Park. The idea was approved.

One central plot of land of about five acres (Tract #70) has never been purchased (see Figure 4 in Chapter 4). According to William Maughan's February 5, 1959 memorandum related to this tract, "James Mason . . . will not sell . . . has three houses—all near highway and occupied by kinfolks." (At that time, the price for this land would have been about $300 per acre; today it might be $150,000 per acre.)

At the Foundation's May 10, 1961 meeting, Davis reported that $1.3 million had been borrowed from eight banks and eight insurance companies and that the Foundation's outstanding obligations were cleared. Specifically, on March 14, 1961, the 5,051 shares had been redeemed at $111 per share;[15] the Wachovia mortgage had been retired; Tract #52 had been purchased from Hill; and other smaller tracts of land had also been purchased. The remainder of the $1.3 million was to be used to sustain the operations of the Park.

While 1960 began with the sad news of Robbins's death, it ended with the celebration linked to the dedication of the Hanes Building on December 16.[16] In between these extreme events were other highs and lows. Three companies showed interest in the Park that year—Allied Chemical Corporation,[17] Corning Glass Works, and Minute Maid[18]— but none committed. But at the August 4 meeting of the Foundation's executive committee, the first 16.29 acres was given to the Research Triangle Institute for the location of the Dreyfus Laboratory. On November 19, Governor Hodges announced that the U.S. Forest Service would build a biological laboratory in the Park;[19] and on the same day, it was announced that John B. Wilson would build a facility to lease to smaller research companies that wanted to locate in the Park but did not have the financial means to build their own laboratory.

Shea was not as successful in marketing the Park as Moore had hoped. Rather than replace him, the Foundation decided at its November 28, 1961 meeting to open a New York office and to hire Lauchlin M. Currie as director of development of the Research Triangle, effective January 1, 1962.[20] As stated in the minutes, his official responsibility was "to tell the story of the Research Triangle complex and to interest national research corporations in visiting North Carolina and the Park." At best, the New York venture planted some seeds in the minds of corporation officers. The office was closed at the end of 1963.[21]

According to George Herbert (1993), in these lean years, "the Institute, through its research activities . . . , did more to spread the knowl-

Figure 11. *Ground breaking of the Robert M. Hanes Memorial Building, March 1960. Davis is holding an early model of the Hanes Building and Research Triangle campus. Left to right: Archie K. Davis, Ann Hanes Willis, Frank Borden Hanes, Mrs. Robert M. Hanes, Governor Luther H. Hodges.*

edge of the existence of a thing called the Research Triangle than any other effort of advertising. . . . The existence of the Institute was absolutely critical to giving credibility to something that had a name. . . . I'm not sure that the Park would have survived its early years without the success of the Institute . . . and the Institute could not have had that success without the universities." Along these same lines, Little (1993) thinks of Chemstrand as "one anchor and the Institute as the other."

All in all, the first half of the decade was sobering for all concerned. The headquarters of the American Association of Textile Chemists and Colorists committed to a small facility, as did the state, which announced plans to build the North Carolina Science and Technology Research Center.[22] Still, that was not enough.

At the May 13, 1964 meeting of the Foundation's board of directors, Davis reported that he still had not received a final ruling from the IRS regarding the Pinelands company's future tax obligations from the sale of land. Also at that meeting, Moore began discussions about liquidating the two thousand acres south of Route 54, but the issue died quietly.

In August 1965, Ned E. Huffman became executive vice president.[23] During his tenure (1965 to 1988), a significant number of organizations were established in the Park, as shown in Appendix B. According to Aycock (1993), "he was a remarkable salesman."

Although times were lean, the leadership never questioned the vision of Archie Davis or doubted that the venture was going to be a success.[24] According to Friday (1993), "We were saying to ourselves, well, we've made this investment, we've built this structure, we've got this property, and we've got to make this work, so where are we not doing what we need to be doing? It was a reassessment time to be sure. . . . [but] there was never a time when we lost faith in the project."

# CHAPTER 8

# CEASING TO BE PIONEERS

*What's past is prologue.*
—WILLIAM SHAKESPEARE

## 27709

The events of 1965 marked the turning point for the Park. The wisdom and leadership of such men as George Simpson and Archie Davis had brought the Park to this pivotal point. Several major organizations committed to the Research Triangle that year. As a result, not only did the Park achieve national visibility, but the state also began to realize its contribution to the economy.

One noteworthy event took place rather quietly. On the morning of August 26, the Research Triangle Park received its own zip code—27709! According to Elizabeth Aycock (1992), who had picked up the mail from the Raleigh-Durham airport since 1960, "on that day we ceased to be pioneers."[1]

## NATIONAL INSTITUTE OF ENVIRONMENTAL HEALTH SCIENCES

Governor Terry Sanford announced on his last day in office, January 6, 1965, that the U.S. Department of Health, Education, and Welfare (HEW) had selected Research Triangle Park for its $70 million Environmental Health Sciences Center. (Today this organization is known as the National Institute of Environmental Health Sciences.) This announcement marked the end of a three-and-a-half-year effort to obtain that facility.

On January 11, 1965, the *Raleigh News and Observer* reported, "The tangled tale of how North Carolina finally wound up as the site for the big federal environmental health center reads like a 'who-dunit.'" The paper was right.

In June 1961, Charles Weiss of the School of Public Health at the University of North Carolina at Chapel Hill was attending a professional meeting in Michigan when he first learned that HEW was planning to build a national facility for research on environmental health. That August, Emil T. Chanlett, also from the School of Public Health, heard about the project when he was on reserve military duty in Washington, D.C. Chanlett mentioned the government's plans to his colleague Daniel A. Okun.[2] Chanlett and Okun then urged both Pearson Stewart and Chancellor William B. Aycock to try to attract the facility to the Park.

Chancellor Aycock took the idea to President William Friday, who authorized the faculty members to write a memorandum to HEW on the advantages of North Carolina.[3] On October 19, 1961, they wrote to HEW and all of North Carolina's congressmen, stressing the availability of land in the Triangle area, its convenient access to Washington, and the availability of academic resources and manpower.

Weiss and Chanlett later took their idea to Governor Sanford. Agreeing that North Carolina should compete for the facility, Sanford enlisted the help of Oscar Ewing. Ewing had served as administrator of the Federal Security Agency (which later became HEW) during two previous administrations. Having retired in Chapel Hill, Ewing was a member of the Research Triangle Regional Planning Commission and was on the board of directors of the Research Triangle Foundation. He quickly learned that forty-six other states were also lobbying for the center.

Governor Sanford wrote to Senator Lister Hill, an Alabama Democrat and ranking member on the Senate Appropriations Committee, on April 20, 1962. He outlined in his letter the advantages that North Carolina offered, noted explicitly that construction costs in North Carolina were significantly less than in the Washington area, and offered the government free land in the Park for the center. Sanford sent a similar letter to the Bureau of the Budget. For nearly a year, there was very little news. Then, in early 1963, the unofficial word came that Anthony J. Celebrezze, secretary of HEW, favored locating the center on a four-hundred-acre site in Beltsville, Maryland.[4] In response, Governor Sanford and Ewing visited the White House to talk with President Kennedy.

Sanford had seconded Kennedy's presidential nomination at the 1960 Democratic Convention, and Ewing had known Kennedy since he was a little boy. They received Kennedy's assurance that the center would go to North Carolina (Aycock 1992). The *Durham Sun* reported on July 30, 1963, that no decision had been reached on the location of the Environmental Health Center but that the White House had instructed Celebrezze "not to push for construction in [the Beltsville] area."

On September 9, 1964, the *Washington Post* reported that the Senate and House Conference Committee voted $1 million to plan for the Environmental Health Center but that the center could not be built within fifty miles of Washington. Later, it was learned that this fifty-mile provision had been added to the appropriations bill by Senator Robert C. Byrd of West Virginia in an effort to attract the center to his state.

On the morning of January 6, 1965, the Foundation heard that North Carolina might lose the center. Shortly thereafter, Hodges placed a call to Celebrezze,[5] and that afternoon the official word was given that the center would definitely come to the Research Triangle Park (Aycock 1992). Kennedy's earlier promise to Sanford and Ewing had been kept.

Governor Dan Moore honored Sanford's earlier recruiting promise that land would be given to the government for the center. On March 18, 1965, it was announced that the General Assembly, in response to a request from the Council of State (the governor plus seven elected state department heads), had approved a $750,000 unconditional grant to the Research Triangle Foundation. This grant was considered payment for the 509 acres of land that the Foundation had given the federal government for the Environmental Health Center (Aycock 1992).

In the spring of 1965, Surgeon General Luther Terry visited the

Park. He sought temporary headquarters so that the center could begin its research while its laboratory was being planned and constructed. The Triangle Service Center was incorporated in June 1965. The Foundation conveyed two parcels of land to this subsidiary organization. The Service Center constructed eight buildings and leased them to the government in June 1966.

## IBM

On April 14, 1965, Governor Moore joined IBM officials to announce that IBM would locate a 600,000-square-foot research facility on four hundred acres in the Park.

IBM had been courted for seven years. Much of the activity related to this process had been kept a secret. In the summer of 1964, Wisner Miller, the real estate representative for IBM, "unexpectedly showed up at the Foundation" (Aycock 1992). The only person in the office that afternoon was Elizabeth Aycock. She showed him maps of the Park and contacted Governor Hodges, but the day ended uneventfully. Shortly thereafter, IBM sent Andy Randino to study the area. His activities were a well-kept secret.[6] All of the materials that he requested—regarding schools, housing, cultural activities—were sent to his home so as not to alert any IBM employees of IBM's interest. Then, out of the blue, IBM called and said that they would be in the Park on April 14 to announce their intention to build a research facility for the IBM 360 model computer.

The Pinelands minutes from August 24, 1965, show that 369.188 acres were conveyed to IBM on August 10, 1965. At $2,200 per acre, Aycock (1992) explained, this sale gave the Foundation sufficient funds to pay off its mortgage. In fact, "we could send out for some black ink because we'd been operating in the red for so long." On August 31, 1965, the Pinelands Company, Inc., was liquidated by the Research Triangle Foundation, as Archie Davis had long planned.

The acreage that IBM wanted was in part occupied by the Durham County Wildlife Club. A relocation agreement was reached: the Foundation bought the club's thirty acres and gave them ninety-five acres plus $105,000 to relocate in the southern part of the Park.

"IBM was the turning point," according to Archie Davis (1992).

Figure 12. *Burning of the Research Triangle Foundation's mortgage in the Hanes Building, November 1965.* Left to right: *Governor Luther H. Hodges, Elizabeth Aycock, G. Akers Moore, Jr., Oscar R. Ewing, Donald B. Anderson, Thomas W. Alexander, Archie K. Davis, Ned E. Huffman.*

Not only was the Foundation now free of debt, but IBM's presence also validated the mission of the Park.[7]

## AND THERE WAS MORE TO COME

Amid the excitement and notoriety of the Environmental Health Center and IBM, it was easy to overlook the smaller, yet equally important new tenants.[8] Technitrol, Inc., a Philadelphia-based computer electronics research company, committed to move into the Park. And the ground-breaking for the headquarters of the North Carolina State Board of Science and Technology had been scheduled.

As a precursor to other activities and organizations that would enhance the region through the universities, the Triangle Universities Computation Center (TUCC) was established with a $50,000 grant from the Board of Science and Technology. Its purpose was to provide educational and computing resources for the state's universities.

On the vision of Archie Davis, the Foundation established the Triangle Service Center in June 1965. Davis, who, like Simpson, never doubted the Park's ultimate success, believed that the Foundation needed to ensure itself of income in perpetuity once all of its land was sold. Toward this end, the Triangle Service Center would be a tax-paying corporation, located on two tracts of land deeded by the Foundation. There it would build rental buildings (and eventually restaurants, banks, and other services needed by employees in the Park).

Also, Beaunit Fibers, a division of Beaunit Corporation, announced in October that it would build a $5 million, 50,000-square-foot research facility on one hundred acres.[9]

Appendix B lists, by year established, the organizations that are, or have been, located in the Park. Also, a comparison of the Park in 1965 with the Park in 1994 clearly shows tremendous growth. See Figures 13 and 14.

Each organization in the Park makes a unique contribution to the mission of the Research Triangle and to the state. However, one organization needs to be singled out, because its creation, initiated by Archie Davis and William Friday, underscored both the vision and the generosity of mind and spirit that has characterized the Research Triangle.

In the early 1970s, forward-looking Davis realized that the Park was running out of large tracts of land. He thought the Foundation should give one tract of land to the three universities so that they would have a permanent home in the Park and be a reminder to all of their role in the creation of the Park. Davis asked President Friday to chair a committee to devise such a plan. In 1975, the Foundation deeded 120 acres to the Triangle Universities Center for Advanced Studies, Inc. (TUCASI). TUCASI's articles of incorporation state, "The purpose of this corporation shall be to assist in and facilitate the planning and execution of non-profit research and educational programs that utilize and enhance the productivity of the intellectual and physical resources of the University of North Carolina at Chapel Hill, Duke University in Durham, and North Carolina State University in Raleigh."

Just as the universities had been crucial in early years, acting as magnets to pull research companies into the Park, their importance would be realized yet again.

The American Academy of Arts and Sciences in Boston was looking for a location to create a National Humanities Center. The unique three-university consortium represented by TUCASI focused the academy's attention on the Triangle. At the invitation of President Friday, Davis and other university members met representatives of the academy for dinner in Chapel Hill. Impressed with both the integrity of the Research Triangle and the commitment of the universities to having the National Humanities Center in the Park, the center came in 1978. The universities each committed $75 thousand per year over five years for the operating costs of the center, which would be located on TUCASI's land. Archie Davis raised the $2.6 million for construction of the center's building in only thirty-two days (Aycock 1993).

What had passed was prologue. The Research Triangle was conceived as an economic development plan to increase employment opportunities and to diversify the North Carolina economy. By the end of 1965, all indications were that it was a success.[10]

Over the years, the disparate opinions and desires of many groups —the universities, the land developers, those in public office—had been reconciled for the common good of the state. George Simpson's reflections on the history of the Research Triangle, some thirty years after it all began, tell the whole story:

> Looking back now, it seems so obvious that all these groups had a lot to gain by working together. But back then it wasn't so obvious. . . . What it took was the willingness of public-spirited leaders from various segments of the community to downplay their differences. There was a great generosity of spirit that dominated from the beginning, and this was what enabled people to look beyond their own narrow interests for the benefit of the entire project. From this generosity came first a basic agreement to work together. Once that was reached, the positive aspects of working together . . . took over and we were on our way. (Franco 1985, p. 165)

This generosity of spirit is the history of the Research Triangle Park.

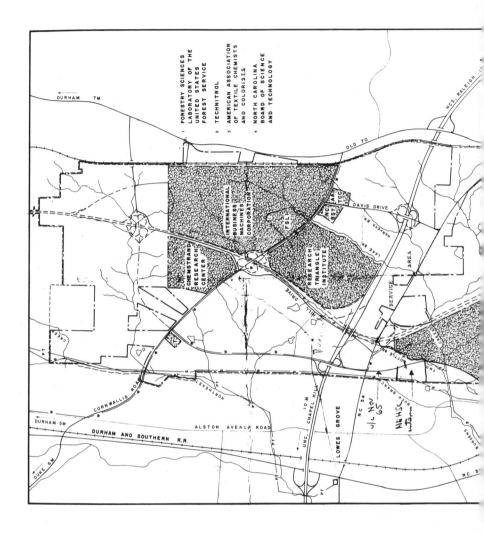

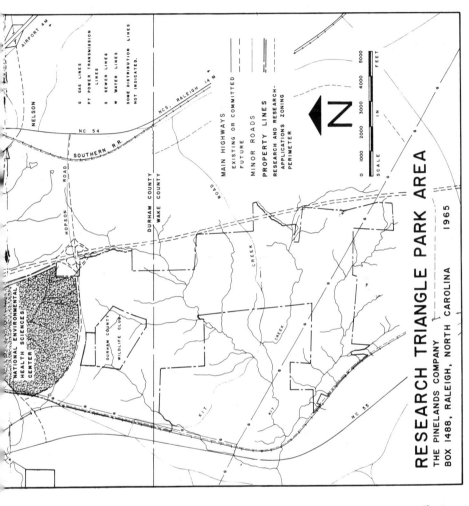

Figure 13. *Map of Research Triangle Park, 1965.*

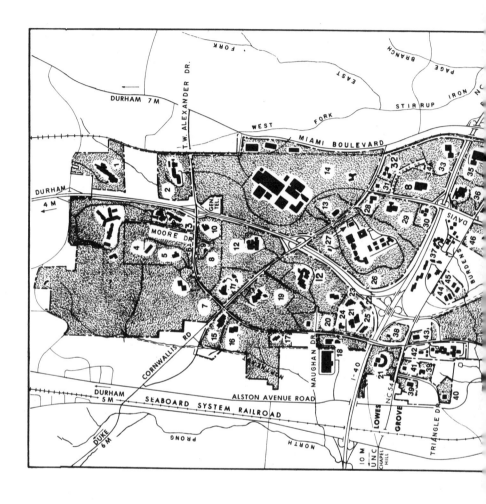

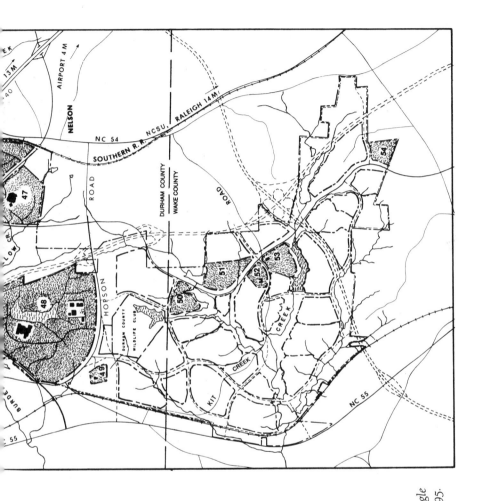

Figure 14. *Map of Research Triangle Park, 1995.*

# FIRST BROCHURE OF
# THE RESEARCH TRIANGLE
# COMMITTEE, INC.
# (DECEMBER 1956)

# The Research Triangle of North Carolina

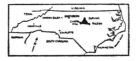

The Research Triangle consists of —

**The University of North Carolina in Chapel Hill,**

**Duke University in Durham,**

**North Carolina State College of Agriculture and Engineering in Raleigh.**

These three institutions exist in a small triangular area in the heart of the state. From a point in the center of this triangle it is no more than fifteen miles to any one of the institutions.

**The University of North Carolina and Duke University are members of the Association of American Universities.**

**North Carolina State College, a part of the Consolidated University of North Carolina, is one of the leading technical schools of the Nation and a member of the American Association of Land Grant Colleges and Universities.**

More than 850 research people on the staffs of these three institutions are currently at work. Their interests range from the most abstract mathematical formulations to the immediate and practical problems of the farmer or the manufacturer.

The combined library facilities number more than two million volumes. Virtually every scientific periodical is available, and listed in a published checklist.

Currently, a total of more than $7,000,000 is budgeted for organized research. These funds come from the operational budgets of the three institutions, from grants by government and industry, and from contracts with government and industry.

**This concentration of research people and facilities in the Research Triangle is one of several in the Nation; it is unique in the South.**

# Natural Development

The Research Triangle was not planned. As in the Boston area, these schools developed separately as educational institutions. Their research programs are based upon the fundamental subject matter areas. The faculties have been chosen for their strength in basic scientific knowledge.

**The name "RESEARCH TRIANGLE", therefore, crystallizes the past growth and present excellence of these three institutions that have grown up so close together.**

But, more than this, the name "RESEARCH TRIANGLE" reflects certain realities of the present and future:

**Research is the vital element in industrial development.**

**Research rests on two bases. One basis is the individual— the lonely seeker after truth. He is the main mover in fundamental scientific progress. The other basis is the concentration of research facilities — laboratories and libraries — and the working and talking together of scientists of many sorts. Both bases are found in the Research Triangle.**

**The conversion of scientific knowledge to industrial use requires a concentration of many subsidiary talents and services: technicians and machine shops, for instance. These are on the increase in the Triangle area.**

**The industrial development of the South is based on science. This great region holds vast potentials of production and marketing. Research and the application of research are making this potential come alive. The future is opening wide for the region.**

**The framework for a modern industrial research complex has been developed soundly in the Research Triangle of North Carolina.**

# The Atmosphere of Research

**Research is no lately come thing at any of these three institutions. The tradition of research and free inquiry, as well as the practice, has developed over many years.**

The University of North Carolina, the oldest state university, has long been known for its research — in both the social and natural sciences. In the latter, special strength is found in chemistry and the biological sciences. Mathematics and mathematical statistics constitute a strong companion area. A major new development at Chapel Hill has been the recent establishment of the Institute of Natural Science.

At Duke University, sound research programs have been built in all basic areas. Research there is also symbolized in one of its aspects by the Duke Medical School and teaching hospital. The Duke medical complex has led decisively in the state and region. Or, again, the basic research program of the Ordnance Corps of the Army is administered near the Duke campus.

North Carolina State College was established in 1889 for two major purposes: (1) to train young men in the agricultural and technical sciences: and (2) to carry on research in these areas, especially research that bore directly on the needs of North Carolina industry and agriculture. From the beginning research in agriculture has been outstanding, supported liberally by state and federal governments, and by local agricultural interests. Within the past twenty years there has been an almost breathtaking growth of research in industrial areas—in engineering, textiles, forest products, for example.

Scientists of industrial laboratories, such as that of the American Machine and Foundry Company at Raleigh, find the Triangle area congenial and stimulating.

# Selected Areas of Training And Research

**The Institute of Statistics.**

There are branches at both the University of North Carolina and North Carolina State College of this world famous Institute. Among the areas of specialization are industrial statistics, probability theory, biological statistics.

**Engineering.**

At Duke University: Civil, Electrical and Mechanical. At North Carolina State College: Ceramic, Chemical, Civil, Electrical, Mechanical, Nuclear, Geological, Metallurgical and Industrial.

WINSTON SALEM

GREENS

**Medical Training and Biological Sciences.**

At Duke University: School of Medicine, Duke Teaching Hospital, School of Nursing. At the University of North Carolina: School of Medicine, North Carolina Memorial Teaching Hospital, School of Nursing, School of Dentistry, School of Pharmacy, School of Public Health. More than 200 full time faculty people in the basic areas of Zoology and Botany, and in the special areas ranging from CHARLOTTE to plant pathology.

UNIVER

ASHEVILLE

**Nuclear Training and Research.**

At North Carolina State College: Nuclear reactor, training program in nuclear engineering.
At Duke University: a 4,000,000 volt Van de Graaf accelerator.
At all three institutions, course work basic to this field.

**Libraries.**

More than two million volumes in the combined libraries, including virtually all scientific periodicals. A checklist of scientific publications is available. There are numerous departmental libraries. Library of Congress catalogues are available at all three libraries.

**Chemistry.**

More than 65 faculty people in chemistry, chemical engineering, and biological chemistry. Extensive laboratory facilities exist.

**The Social Sciences.**

Outstanding are the Institute for Research in Social Science and the Psychometric Laboratory of the University in Chapel Hill. There are also excellent facilities in business administration and industrial psychology.

# An Area For Training

Degree programs at the three institutions cover a wide range of basic and applied science fields.

The Research Triangle area offers a substantial annual crop of young men and women with both baccalaureate and graduate degrees. As opportunities for employment at home increase, their numbers will increase. Approximate current enrollments in a few selected areas are as follows:

| | Undergraduate | Graduate |
|---|---|---|
| Chemistry | 250 | 100 |
| Chemical Engineering, etc. | 205 | 26 |
| Physics | 90 | 65 |
| Nuclear Engineering | 240 | 40 |
| Engineering Physics | 25 | 1 |
| Mathematics | 49 | 36 |
| Statistics | | 56 |
| Textiles | 195 | 17 |
| Botany and Zoology | 123 | 82 |
| Electrical Engineering | 875 | 20 |
| Total Enrollment in Schools of Engineering | 3,400 | 150 |

Consistent with their resources and educational responsibilities, the three institutions offer programs of graduate study for off-campus students. All such programs go through the normal channels of academic approval.

The state of North Carolina is currently getting underway a program of building technical schools, for training in industrial skills beyond the high school level.

# The State And The Region

The Research Triangle has a particular relevance to the present economic situation in North Carolina, and in the South as a whole.

**North Carolina was the pioneer state of the South in industrial development. This early start brought eventual predominance in the tobacco industry, as well as a major portion of the furniture and textile industry of the nation.**

The South, it is well known, has during the past quarter century made a major industrial breakthrough — indeed the whole life of the region has changed.

North Carolina and the South have unmistakably come of age industrially. In the past, most of the research and service necessities of industry have been borrowed from other parts of the Nation.

The industrial component of the region is now large enough to require and justify the location of major research and industrial service activities within the region — a regional research center comparable to those in the East, the Midwest and the Far West.

Largely because of her early industrial progress, North Carolina was able to build and support the University and North Carolina State College at high levels of academic work. At Duke, a great endowment based on tobacco manufacture was added to a good college, and Duke has come quickly and soundly to the upper levels of university work.

North Carolina, the largest industrial state in the South, is now ready for the second great stage in her industrial development, and to take the lead in supplying the research core for the region.

# A Place To Live

The Research Triangle area provides a combination of the large bustling metropolitan world, and the quiet pools of life on the small scale.

Durham is an industrial and commercial city of seventy-five thousand population. Raleigh is a political, commercial, and industrial center of eighty thousand people. Chapel Hill remains in large part "academe among the trees".

There is thus enough size to provide excellent shopping facilities. Transportation is good. Two main North-South railroads serve the area, with excellent overnight transportation to Washington and New York. The Raleigh-Durham Airport is almost exactly in the center of the Triangle. It is served competitively by several major airlines, 35 flights leaving daily.

Concerts are frequent by national touring artists and companies; indeed, during the season there is scarcely a week when some excellent program is not available. Many national companies of New York plays come to the area. In sports, there are those who say that there is too great a supply. Speakers of national and international stature appear frequently on the campuses.

**At the same time, the Triangle area does not have the disadvantages of congested metropolitan areas. Quiet suburban developments are the rule, and there is virtually unlimited area for expansion. Good roads serve the whole area.**

The faculties and their families of the three institutions constitute major parts of the life of all three towns, so that the general population has for many years accepted them on their own terms. There is a friendly, sympathetic atmosphere in which research people may live and work.

In the Triangle area itself, and in nearby areas, there is a great concentration of colleges and universities. With two teaching hospitals and several other hospitals, medical facilities are outstanding.

The public schools are adequate, and there is a pervasive sentiment for their improvements.

# The Governor's Research Triangle Committee, Inc.

George L. Simpson, Jr., Director, Box 1488, Raleigh, N. C.

The Governor's Research Triangle Committee, Incorporated, is a non-stock, non-profit organization whose purpose is to do all that is possible to use and develop the research resources of the Triangle area.

The Committee works solely within the bounds and desires of the three institutions. Its primary purpose is to make industrial and governmental research activities aware of the scientific resources and cultural advantages of the Triangle area.

When asked, the Committee will undertake to arrange a meeting between such industrial and governmental agencies and appropriate people from the three institutions.

The Committee undertakes also to help in carrying forward any projects deemed desirable by one or more of the institutions.

## MEMBERS

Robert M. Hanes, President. Honorary Chairman of Board, Wachovia Bank and Trust Company, Winston-Salem, N. C.

A. Hollis Edens, Vice President. President, Duke University, Durham, N. C.

Brandon P. Hodges, Secretary-Treasurer. Counselor, The Champion Paper and Fibre Company, Canton, N. C.

Luther H. Hodges, Governor of North Carolina, Raleigh, N. C.

William C. Friday, President, University of North Carolina, Chapel Hill, N. C.

Robert Armstrong, Vice President, Celanese Corporation of America, Charlotte, N. C.

E. Y. Floyd, Director, N. C. Plant Food Institute, Raleigh, N. C.

Grady Rankin, Attorney, Gastonia, N. C.

C. W. Reynolds, Asst. Works Mgr., Western Electric Company, Winston-Salem, N. C.

William H. Ruffin, President, Erwin Mills, Durham, N. C.

## WORKING COMMITTEE

J. Harold Lampe, Dean, School of Engineering, N. C. State College, Chairman.

W. C. Davison, Dean, School of Medicine, Duke University

Marcus E. Hobbs, Dean, Graduate School, Duke University

D. W. Colvard, Dean, School of Agriculture, N. C. State College

Henry T. Clark, Jr., Administrator, Division of Health Affairs, University of N. C.

W. J. Seeley, Dean, College of Engineering, Duke University

Arthur Roe, Director of the Institute of Natural Science, University of N. C.

Malcolm Campbell, Dean, School of Textiles, N. C. State College

Gordon W. Blackwell, Director of The Institute for Research in Social Science, University of N. C.

# APPENDIX B

# ORGANIZATIONS LOCATED IN THE PARK: PAST AND PRESENT

| Organization | Year Established |
|---|---|
| Research Triangle Foundation of North Carolina | 1959 |
| Research Triangle Institute | 1959 |
| Chemstrand Research Center, Inc. | 1960 |
| *Name changed to "Monsanto" in 1974; left in 1984; property sold to Burroughs Wellcome Company* | |
| U.S. Department of Agriculture–Forest Service | 1962 |
| American Association of Textile Chemists and Colorists | 1964 |
| Technitrol, Inc. | 1965 |
| *Left in 1972; property bought by Troxler Electronic Laboratories, Inc.* | |
| N.C. Science & Technology Research Center | 1965 |
| *Left in 1991* | |
| International Business Machines Corporation (IBM) | 1966 |
| National Institute of Environmental Health Sciences (NIEHS) | 1966 |
| National Center for Health Statistics | 1966 |
| Triangle Universities Computation Center (TUCC) | 1966 |
| *Left in 1990* | |
| UNC General Administration–Network Services | 1966 |
| *Formerly N.C. Educational Computing Service* | |

| Organization | *Year Established* |
|---|---|
| Beaunit Corporation | 1967 |
| *Left in 1975; property leased to EPA; property sold to JHPB in 1978* | |
| Hercules, Inc. | 1967 |
| *Left in 1978; property leased to IBM* | |
| Burroughs Wellcome Company | 1970 |
| *Bought by Glaxo, Inc., in 1995* | |
| U.S. Environmental Protection Agency | . 1971 |
| Becton, Dickinson and Company Research Center | 1973 |
| Mantech Environmental Technology, Inc. | 1974 |
| *Formerly Northrup Services, Inc., and NSI* | |
| Troxler Electronic Laboratories, Inc. | 1974 |
| Triangle Universities Center for Advanced Studies, Inc. (TUCASI) | 1975 |
| U.S. Army Research Office | 1975 |
| *Left in 1984* | |
| International Fertility Research Program | 1976 |
| *Name changed to Family Health International in 1982; left in 1988* | |
| BOC Gases | 1977 |
| *Formerly Airco Special Gases and Electronic Development Facility* | |
| Data General Corporation | 1977 |
| Research Commons (owned by JHPB) | 1978 |
| *Includes former Beaunit property* | |
| Computer Sciences Corporation | 1978 |
| National Humanities Center | 1978 |
| NIEHS–National Toxicology Program | 1978 |
| North Carolina State Education Assistance Authority | 1978 |
| Chemical Industry Institute of Toxicology | 1979 |
| UNC Institute for Transportation Research and Education (ITRE) | 1979 |
| *Left in 1989* | |
| J.E. Sirrine Company | 1979 |
| *Left in 1987; property bought by Burroughs Wellcome in 1987* | |
| Battelle | 1980 |
| Compuchem Environmental Corporation | 1980 |
| Compuchem Laboratories, Inc. | 1980 |
| ISA (Instrument Society of America) | 1980 |

| Organization | Year Established |
|---|---|
| MCNC | 1980 |
| *Formerly Microelectronics Center of North Carolina* | |
| NorTel | 1980 |
| *Formerly Northern Telecom, Inc.* | |
| Rhone-Poulenc AG Company | 1980 |
| *Formerly Union Carbide Agricultural Products Company, Inc.* | |
| Radian Corporation | 1980 |
| *Left in 1994* | |
| GE Microelectronics Center | 1981 |
| *Left in 1989; property bought by Harris Semiconductor in 1989* | |
| Dyncorp | 1981 |
| *Formerly Program Resources, Inc.; left in 1995* | |
| North Carolina Biotechnology Center | 1982 |
| Semiconductor Research Corporation (SRC) | 1982 |
| Glaxo, Inc. | 1983 |
| *Name changed to Glaxo Wellcome Inc., in 1995* | |
| GTE Systems | 1983 |
| Sumitomo Electric Lightwave Corporation | 1983 |
| Triangle Research Collaborative, Inc. (TRC) | 1983 |
| Ciba–Agricultural Biotechnology Research Unit | 1984 |
| *Formerly Ciba-Geigy* | |
| Kobe Steel USA, Inc. | 1984 |
| DuPont Electronics Technology Center | 1985 |
| UAI Technology, Inc. | 1985 |
| BASF Corporation Agricultural Products | 1986 |
| Cedalion Systems, Inc. | 1986 |
| The Glaxo Foundation | 1986 |
| Underwriters Laboratories, Inc. | 1986 |
| BNR Inc. (Bell Northern Research) | 1987 |
| Triangle Universities Licensing Corporation (TULCO) | 1988 |
| *Transferred functions to universities in 1995* | |
| Harris Semiconductor | 1989 |
| *Bought by Motorola in 1994* | |
| Litespec, Inc. | 1989 |

| Organization | Year Established |
|---|---|
| McMahan Biotechnology | 1989 |
| McMahan Electro-Optics, Inc. | 1989 |
| Mobius Group, Inc. | 1989 |
| The University of North Carolina Center for Public Television | 1989 |
| Ericsson, Inc. | 1990 |
| *Formerly Ericsson GE Mobile Communications, Inc.* | |
| National Institute of Statistical Sciences | 1990 |
| Reichhold Chemicals, Inc. | 1990 |
| Sigma Xi, The Scientific Research Society | 1990 |
| Kyushu Matsushita Electric Research Laboratory (KMERL)–Panasonic Technologies, Inc. | 1991 |
| First Flight Venture Center | 1991 |
| Governor's Institute on Alcohol and Substance Abuse, Inc. | 1991 |
| North Carolina Technological Development Authority, Inc. | 1991 |
| Silentpower Technologies, Inc. | 1991 |
| JMC (USA), Inc. | 1992 |
| Martin Marietta Corporation | 1992 |
| Motor and Equipment Manufacturers Association | 1992 |
| Datawatch Corporation, Triangle Software Division | 1993 |
| *Left in 1995* | |
| Medco Research, Inc. | 1993 |
| NJC Enterprises, Ltd. | 1993 |
| Cisco Systems, Inc. | 1994 |
| Duke Mass Spectrometry Facility | 1994 |
| Motorola MOS-15 | 1994 |
| NetEdge Systems, Inc. | 1994 |
| Novel Pharmaceutical, Inc./1-800-9-Analysis, Inc. | 1994 |
| *Separate companies in same location* | |
| Biogen, Inc. | 1995 |
| Corning BioPro | 1995 |

# NOTES

1. This statement was written by George L. Simpson, Jr., the first director of the Research Triangle Committee, Inc. (the predecessor to today's Research Triangle Foundation). It appeared in a special section of the *New York Times* on November 11, 1957.

2. It appears from written records that the term "Research Triangle" was first recorded in Romeo H. Guest's appointment book with reference to an October 10, 1953 meeting with Robert A. Armstrong, director of research at Celanese Corporation. According to Guest (1979), at that time he was thinking in terms of the general area defined by the three universities. Many writers and commentators on the Research Triangle credit Guest with the first use of the term (see Chapter 1), and a few even go so far as to credit him with the initial Triangle idea.

3. North Carolina State College became North Carolina State University in 1965 (Reagan 1987).

4. The universities were directly involved in planning, implementing, building, and promoting the Research Triangle. Their involvement was critical to the success of the Park (Herbert 1993).

5. Other writers have attempted to assign Odum credit for the Research Triangle idea (e.g., Wilson 1967; Franco 1985). However, based on discussions with some of those directly involved in the planning at the time (e.g., Simpson 1991; Newell 1992), I question the hypothesis that there was a direct relation-

ship between Odum's ideas and the original Triangle concept. There certainly was an important indirect relationship: Simpson was a student of Odum's.

6. Simpson also used this phrase to describe why the Park was a success. For example, he wrote that the "single most important aspect of the Research Triangle was the generosity of mind exhibited by all elements involved" (Simpson 1988, p. 1).

7. According to George Herbert (1993), the first president of the Research Triangle Institute, when the state's leadership "decided that something was good for North Carolina and they were going to make it happen, they stuck with it and they made it happen."

CHAPTER 1 *The Idea Takes Shape*

1. Walter W. Harper was a student at State College in the late 1940s. From his experiences as a student worker in the Engineering Research Department, he recalled that faculty would frequently chat about "utilizing research to help build a more diversified industrial base" (Harper 1992).

2. Harper (1992) recalled one incident that took place in early 1954. As assistant director of foundations at State College, he was testing the often-mentioned idea that the universities (State College, in particular) could be a magnet to attract new industry to the state. With this goal in mind, he met with Ollie Greenway, president of International Resistors Corporation in Philadelphia, a company that was looking at North Carolina as a possible relocation site. Harper was well received by Greenway, who quickly understood the potential benefit of locating near a major university. Unfortunately, the company did not select North Carolina for their location.

From Harper's perspective, Brandon Hodges was one of the first of the North Carolina officials to see and understand the role of universities in economic development. W. Kerr Scott was governor of North Carolina (1949–53) at that time: "He was an agricultural governor. . . . He supported C&D [the Department of Conservation and Development], but he didn't have the personal interest. Brandon really filled that role. He understood education" (Harper 1991).

3. North Carolina established the Department of Conservation and Development on March 1, 1925. One of its missions was to encourage new industry to locate production facilities in the state.

Harper (1991) first met Guest in 1951 in the office of Horace Cotton, director of C&D: "I heard someone say 'H-e-l-l-o t-h-e-r-e, I'm Romeo Guest,' in a little English tone. And I looked up. . . . I'd heard so much about him I thought he was going to be 6' 9" and weigh three hundred pounds and hit the table hard and everything. [He was] very refined; a delicate man, but a real dynamo."

4. Guest's father had been "in industrial construction since before 1893,

[and his] grandfather built power dams to run grist mills" (Colvard 1986). In 1938, Romeo Guest moved from South Carolina to Greensboro, North Carolina (where his sister and her husband lived), in search of new construction opportunities. Readers interested in Guest's early years in construction (before 1940) should see the transcript of a May 9, 1981 meeting with Guest and his former associates (Guest 1981).

5. Other writers on the history of the Research Triangle—for example, Hamilton (1966), Wilson (1967), and the graduate students who have relied on their works, such as Jones (1978) and Franco (1985)—emphasized Guest's first-hand experience in seeing the Route 128 phenomenon develop around Boston as the seed that eventually launched the Research Triangle idea. In his later years, Guest also mentioned these events during interviews.

It is my opinion that the importance of research to industry and the benefits associated with being close to universities was simply "in the air" (Simpson 1991).

6. Guest (1977) recalled that this meeting took place at the Pine Needles Inn in Southern Pines, North Carolina.

7. Merck wanted to produce medicinal chemicals, chemotherapeutic agents, and synthetic vitamins (Guest 1977).

8. Romeo Guest and Brandon Hodges were responsible for attracting Lorillard Tobacco Company to North Carolina, although Guest did not receive the construction contract for that facility (Colvard 1986).

9. According to Harper (1991), Guest was not only generous in sharing his business contacts but was also open with his wealth: "He [Guest] would usually pay. I think we had $7.50 allowance at that time. He'd let me pay the tip and sometimes that was almost more than I could pay."

10. There is no written record of these meetings, but Harper remembers that they took place before he left C&D and moved to Fayetteville in 1953 and before Brandon Hodges left office in June 1953 (Guest 1967; Harper 1992).

11. According to Harper (1991), Brandon Hodges always used the word "hatching." He saw "no reason why we [North Carolina] couldn't hatch our own industry" as opposed to constantly trying to attract industries from other states. From time to time, Horace Cotton, William Guthrie, Richard Mauney, and Edwin Gill would also travel with Guest, Harper, and Brandon Hodges (Jones 1978).

12. Throughout the early discussions, it was implicit that the universities would work to attract research companies rather than manufacturing companies (Harper 1991). At his own expense, Guest visited the Battelle Institute and the Stanford Research Institute in the early 1950s. The earliest written record of these visits is in the daybook of Phyllis Branch Case (then Phyllis Branch) for October 1, 1952, regarding the Stanford Research Institute (Case 1991a). Case was Guest's executive secretary.

13. Guest did meet with Governor Hodges at 10:00 A.M. on December 31,

1954, to discuss the Research Triangle concept. However, the term "Research Triangle" seemed to have been coined by Guest prior to that meeting.

14. Harper (1960) recalled to Case: "In one of our early meetings . . . I remember walking into Mr. Guest's office and he said to me at the outset, 'I have the name for the program.' He said that we were dealing with three institutions and the name *Research Triangle* would be just right for the proposed program." Harper later dated this event as occurring sometime in 1952 (Harper 1992).

15. E. R. Squibb and Sons was one of the first prospects that Guest and Harper visited in the Northeast (Guest 1978).

16. These documents are in the Guest Papers at Duke University, and there are copies in the Research Triangle Foundation archives. See also Jones (1978), Guest (1979), and Larrabee (1992) for more detailed discussions about them. A later reference to Guest's explicit use of the term "Research Triangle" is in a memorandum written by Guest dated June 1, 1954: "Charles Blount, President, United Piece Dye Works, spent the night with Guest. Subject: Research Triangle of North Carolina" (Hamilton 1966; Jones 1978).

17. Milton Fries presented a paper there titled "Research and Industry as a Factor in Southern Development" (Coker 1946). See also Williams (1948).

18. Brandon Hodges left the state treasurer's office in June 1953. At the time of this meeting he was general counsel with Champion Paper and Fiber Company of Canton, North Carolina. Hanes knew Guest from Hanes's capacity as chairman of the Division of Commerce and Industry in the state Department of Conservation and Development. In fact, on previous occasions Hanes had referred Guest to prospective clients (Guest 1977).

19. The final list contained twenty-eight industry leaders from the state and was dated March 6, 1954.

20. This chain of events is inferred from a September 21, 1954 letter from Guest to Brandon Hodges. According to Jones (1978), it was Guest who suggested to Hodges the importance of a meeting with Governor Umstead.

21. Hanes also urged Brandon Hodges to arrange a meeting between Governor Hodges and Guest in late 1954 (Hamilton 1966).

22. Jones (1978) dated these early meetings as having taken place in August 1954, immediately after Harper returned to State College. This date is consistent with Harper's memory of the events.

23. Harper (1992) recalled that the park idea was first mentioned to him by Newell when he, Guest, William P. Saunders, Campbell, and Newell were having dinner at the Sir Walter Hotel in Raleigh in the fall of 1954.

24. Bostian had great regard for both Campbell and Lampe. He described them in very favorable terms: "Campbell . . . He was an operator. . . . Everybody liked Campbell. . . . He was a good drinking buddy of people. . . . He could tell ribald stories, and he was quite a character. But dammit, he was smart too! And he was ready to go with ideas. He had a kind of boldness about

him. Dean Lampe was an extraordinary man. . . . He was a bold thinker. . . . Lampe was an idea man, and a broad-brush thinker. He also had enough energy to follow through on ideas, not just discuss them" (Bostian 1991).

25. By this time, Guest had already met with Lampe about the Triangle idea (Bostian 1991).

26. Both Hamilton (1966) and Jones (1978), who relied in part on Hamilton's research, contend that Brandon Hodges was at this meeting. Others question this point, because Brandon Hodges entered Rex Hospital in Raleigh on December 2 from a heart attack (Guest 1977).

27. Campbell openly acknowledged, as did Newell (1992), that the report was Newell's work (Guest 1976). Newell (1993) did not consult Guest, and Guest did not have any input beyond the ideas he had expressed earlier in Campbell's office. On the cover page of the report Newell wrote: "The contents of this statement are the views of its authors as private citizens, and do not necessarily reflect the opinions of the officials of North Carolina State College or other organizations herein mentioned."

28. Commenting in retrospect on this report, Newell (1993) noted: "Actually, I don't recall that I knew 'many,' although I knew of at least a few, such as Brandon Hodges and Walter Harper. This statement was more of an attempt to distance the document from Romeo Guest's 'commercial' 'Conditioned for Research' brochure, and to put its message into an objective, comprehensive document."

29. Interestingly, Newell did not use the term "Research Triangle" in the report.

30. According to Newell (1989), Guest was given an opportunity to comment by January 7 on an earlier draft of the report, but there are no records of such comments in the Guest Papers, and Guest did not mention any comments during interviews in his later years. Newell (1993) recalled that in later years he received correspondence verifying that Guest did receive a draft of the report.

31. According to Bostian (1991), Governor Hodges had been talking with Brandon Hodges, and it was Brandon Hodges who finally gained the governor's support.

32. According to Guest, "[Brandon Hodges, Harper, Campbell, and I] put our heads together to determine how to sell the research philosophy. I went to Birmingham Research Center in Alabama. They were crowded, with no room for expansion, and had a low budget. I returned with the knowledge obtained from them and proceeded to prepare ['Conditioned for Research']. This is the first printed material on the Research Triangle" (Colvard 1986, p. 6).

Although the brochure is not dated, Jones (1978) carefully investigated its origins. It was printed by the Washburn Printing Company, but no company records were retained from 1954. Correspondence located in the Guest

Papers and dated November 1954 suggests that pamphlet dummies were sent to Thomas T. Evans of Bennett Advertising for text modification and returned to Guest in December 1954.

33. There does not seem to be any question that Guest's initial interest in the Triangle project was based on profit. He thought this project would provide an excellent vehicle for his company to obtain construction contracts. Even in newspaper articles, there was a presumption that Guest would be the contractor for Park buildings. In March 1958, the *Raleigh News and Observer* published an article titled "Guest Is Contractor for Research Park."

34. According to Simpson (1993a), Guest had a "vulnerability that was touching."

35. In later years Guest explained his reluctance to show his material to the governor: "Truthfully, Hodges and I were not close friends" (Colvard 1986, p. 6).

36. Guest's diary in the Guest Papers confirms the December 20 attempted visit, as does a note to Guest from the governor dated December 21. The governor's appointment book also confirms the date and time of this appointment.

37. According to Guest (1980), the meeting with Gordon Gray was arranged by George P. Geoghegan, Jr., of Wachovia Bank and Trust in Raleigh. In a letter dated January 3, 1955, from Gray to Guest, Gray thanked Guest for his visit on December 31, 1954, and enclosed a copy of the so-called Wheeler Report — a report commissioned by Gray to evaluate the physics program at Chapel Hill. John A. Wheeler of Princeton University was on the evaluation committee. Among other things, the report suggested that the three institutions in the area could form the core of a scientific research center in physics (Guest 1977; Jones 1978).

38. This appointment was arranged by Kenneth M. Brim, Guest's attorney from Greensboro. Brim was a graduate of Trinity College and Duke Law School, president of the Duke National Alumni Association, and a trustee on the university's executive committee (Guest 1977).

CHAPTER 2 *Taking the First Step*

1. William S. Guest, son of Romeo Guest, wrote a thesis paper in 1960 as part of his MBA requirements at the University of North Carolina at Chapel Hill. That paper stated: "It is obvious that Mr. X [Romeo Guest] could not carry on such a large promotion job alone. . . . At this point it was decided to establish what is known as the Governor's Research Triangle Committee, Inc." (W. S. Guest 1960, p. 9).

2. According to Walter Harper (1992), Guest started off with a profit motive, but over time he began to view the Research Triangle as something for the good of the state. Phyllis Case (1991a) also remembered that Guest wanted

the project to be a state project all along. William Newell (1992), on the other hand, had the impression that Guest always wanted the Research Triangle to be a private venture, with the state providing only the needed infrastructure. The fact of the matter is that the state did become involved by providing leadership. Later, it also provided some important infrastructural elements.

3. As we will see later, Guest became less involved in those Triangle activities that were related to university participation and more involved in the development side of what was to become the Park. In retrospect, this division of responsibility was probably for the best; Guest did not fully understand the mind-set of the university leadership, and they did not fully understand him or his motives. Case (1991a) would be one of the first to agree that Guest was not always easy to read.

4. It may have been Brandon Hodges who finally pushed the governor to act (Harper 1991).

5. Apparently, President Edens could not attend this meeting. Paul Gross represented Duke University. In a follow-up letter to Guest dated February 10, Bostian wrote that the meeting included R. B. House and W. D. Carmichael from the University of North Carolina and Benjamin Douglas from the Department of Conservation and Development. Bostian was also present (Hamilton 1966; Jones 1978).

According to Jones's research, after this meeting Bostian urged Guest to continue to seek suggestions from the three institutions regarding the content of "Conditioned for Research." Bostian also reported to Guest that the representatives from Chapel Hill expressed skepticism about the likelihood of attracting research facilities to the Triangle area (Jones 1978).

6. It should also be noted that the name of this committee is incorrect in Hodges (1962). I find it interesting that Guest himself, in a series of interviews that began in the late 1970s, did not mention any such organizational proposal, although in an earlier meeting with Hanes he had proposed a similar committee structure. Nevertheless, the organizational structure was formed.

According to Elizabeth Aycock (1991), Hanes went to Germany after World War II to work on the Marshall Plan. He involved Governor Hodges in that project, and the two remained friends thereafter.

7. All individuals were invited to this meeting by telegram. According to the minutes, the council members included the governor; Gordon Gray, president of the University of North Carolina; Hollis Edens, president of Duke University; Grady Rankin from Gastonia; Robert Armstrong, vice president of research at Celanese Corporation in Charlotte; William H. Ruffin, president of Erwin Mills in Durham; E. Y. Floyd, director of the North Carolina–Virginia Plant Food Institute in Raleigh; C. W. Reynolds, assistant works manager at Western Electric Company in Winston-Salem; and Brandon Hodges, general counsel at Champion Paper and Fibre Company in Canton.

8. According to Harper (1991), the governor's involvement was critical

to pulling the three institutions together. He recalled hearing from others that Edens told the governor at this meeting that he was "glad that there was something that he and Carolina [the University] could get together on."

9. The committee's first meeting took place on July 21, 1955, at Riddick Laboratories on the North Carolina State College campus. According to the minutes, the committee also included Gordon W. Blackwell, director of the Institute for research in social sciences at the University of North Carolina at Chapel Hill; R. J. M. Hobbs, dean of the School of Business Administration at Chapel Hill; Henry T. Clark, Jr., administrator of the Division of Health Affairs at Chapel Hill; Marcus E. Hobbs, dean of the graduate school at Duke University; W. C. Davison, dean of the medical school at Duke University; W. J. Seeley, dean of the School of Engineering at Duke University; Dean W. Colvard, dean of the School of Agriculture at State College; and Malcolm E. Campbell, dean of the School of Textiles at State College.

10. The minutes rarely refer to this committee as the Research Triangle Development Committee. It was known by all as the Working Committee.

11. The emphasized statements are from the original minutes. It should be noted that efforts were made for several years to alleviate faculty members' fears and concerns that the Research Triangle would impinge upon their academic missions. Guest was not sensitive to this concern. As I will point out below, the most significant effort toward this end was made by George Simpson.

12. The committee members representing the three institutions were Davison of Duke, Hobbs of Chapel Hill, and Colvard of State College.

13. Other members of this subcommittee were Blackwell of Chapel Hill, Clark of Chapel Hill, and Seeley of Duke.

14. Guest always thought that he was doing something good for North Carolina (as well as for himself), and he did not understand why the universities were reluctant to buy into his plan. Years later, Little (1992) remarked that he had the impression there was simply a suspicious element about Guest. There seemed to be a "reservoir of feeling" within the university [at Chapel Hill] that Guest was trying to push the universities into something they perhaps should not be doing.

15. Several memoranda by members of the Working Committee document that efforts were also being made to identify an executive secretary candidate from searches of *American Men of Science* and similar publications.

16. This effort is also noted in an August 6, 1956 letter from Hanes to Brandon Hodges.

17. As I pointed out in the Introduction, Simpson had been a student of Howard Odum. Simpson was well trained in the various dimensions of regional development and was a very practical person (Hamilton 1966).

18. These individuals were E. A. Clement of Southern Bell Telephone and Telegraph Company; Frank Daniels of the *Raleigh News and Observer*;

James D. Kilgore of Pine State Creamery Company; Guy W. Rawls of Rawls Motor Company; Homer Starling of W. H. King Drug Company; and Gary Underhill of First National Bank (Aycock 1992).

19. The members of the newly incorporated Research Triangle Committee and Working Committee remained approximately the same. William Friday had replaced Gordon Gray. Also, Arthur Roe, director of the Institute of Natural Science at Chapel Hill, had replaced R. J. M. Hobbs, who retired shortly after the inventory report was completed. Hanes had been elected president of the committee.

## CHAPTER 3 *Keeping on the Path*

1. In correspondence and brochures prepared by Simpson, there were numerous references to the Governor's Research Triangle Committee, Inc. The attribution to Governor Hodges in this title was Simpson's idea, not that of the incorporators (Aycock 1991).

2. The *Raleigh News and Observer* reported on October 4, 1956, "Director Moves to Raleigh Research Committee Office."

3. The Supreme Court ruled on the *Brown v. Board of Education* case on May 17, 1954. The ruling stated that in public education, the "separate but equal" concept had no place. Therefore, admission to a public school could not be denied on the basis of race.

4. DuPont moved into the Park in 1985.

5. Simpson knew from the beginning that he would have to visit the larger companies in the region and talk with them about their future research location needs. One of the first things that he and Aycock did was to purchase the National Academy of Sciences' directory of industrial research and development laboratories. This well-used book is still in Aycock's office at the Research Triangle Foundation.

6. According to William Little (1992), "One of the great things that Simpson could do that nobody else, I think, could ever do was to get the heads of the chambers of commerce in Raleigh and Durham to sit down in the same room and act like gentlemen toward each other."

7. There are no records of the amount of money raised at this meeting; however, the bank statement for the Research Triangle Committee, Inc., showed a balance of $9,720.16 on October 31, 1956. Also, in a November 1, 1956 letter to Simpson, George Geoghegan reported collecting about $12,000 from the September 25 luncheon in Raleigh, $5,000 of which went to buy Simpson's car.

8. The first draft of the brochure was typed by Aycock. She remembered typing it late one afternoon and then rushing it to the train station so that Simpson could revise it while on a trip to New York City (Aycock 1992).

9. It is my opinion that Simpson's perception about how the committee

and, later, the Park were to interact with the three institutions illustrates that he was what could be called a man of vision. He just seemed to sense how each step should be taken, and when.

10. Simpson wrote to Governor Hodges on November 6, 1956, asking him to consider calling this January meeting. He wrote, "I feel that I have encountered most of the problems which we face, and that I have a reasonably good idea of how to begin our systematic presentation of the Research Triangle." In a little more than a month, Simpson had digested the work of the earlier groups and set forth a vision to challenge the minds and imaginations of the leaders of North Carolina.

11. One of the first research companies that Simpson visited was Union Carbide. As he described the visit, "We were testing the waters. No one laughed; it was encouraging; people received us seriously" (Simpson 1991).

12. By mid-January, Simpson had talked with the editor of *Industrial Laboratories*, who agreed to write an article about the Triangle. The article appeared that April. Plans were being made for other advertisements as well. In November 1957, an advertising supplement appeared in the *New York Times*.

13. Allied Chemical never located in the Triangle, but the company once held an option on a parcel of land.

14. Some believed that Governor Hodges still did not fully understand the concept that was unfolding. According to Saunders, the governor had thought about purchasing fifty or so acres around State College to attract groups such as testing laboratories to the area (Guest 1981). As energetic as he was, Hodges was a textile man and did not really understand research (Harper 1992).

15. Gross initially mentioned the institute concept to Guest at the January 4, 1955 meeting with representatives from Duke University (Jones 1978). See Chapter 1.

16. Other members of this planning committee included Robert Armstrong, Paul Gross, Harold Lampe, C. W. Reynolds, and William M. Whyburn, the Consolidated University's vice president for research and graduate studies.

17. The Statistics Research Division at the Research Triangle Institute received its first commercial contract—from Union Carbide Nuclear, for $1,138—only eleven months after being established (Herbert 1994). This contract was quickly followed by a second project, this one for $10,000 (Larrabee 1992).

18. A number of significant organizational changes were announced on January 9, 1959, at the Sir Walter Hotel in Raleigh (see Chapter 6).

19. This memorandum is reproduced in full in Larrabee (1992). It should be emphasized that the stated mission of the Institute remained in concert with the early economic development objectives of the Research Triangle.

20. Herbert was hired effective December 1, 1958. Watts Hill initially provided office space for the Institute in Durham (Aycock 1991). Readers

interested in more details should see Larrabee's excellent history of the Institute (1992).

21. It is my opinion that such insight into the thinking of academics was a hallmark of Simpson's tenure as director. A nonacademic, such as Guest, might have been insensitive to the concerns of faculty and thus might have alienated one of the Triangle's greatest resources.

22. Paul Gross was an important liaison to the Duke faculty. According to Marcus Hobbs, Gross "did a tremendous service in helping to demonstrate that scientific research should not always be seen as an end in itself. In some ways, he showed that applied research can play an important role in the university setting" (Franco 1985, p. 143).

On February 21, 1957, in an editorial called "Lopsided Triangle," the *Raleigh News and Observer* pointed out the inconsistency of building a research triangle around three great universities while at the same time cutting the library budgets at the two state universities back to their 1953 levels.

CHAPTER 4 *Pinelands*

1. Governor Hodges and Saunders became friends while they attended the University of North Carolina at Chapel Hill. Saunders (class of 1921) was on the baseball team, and Hodges (class of 1919) was the team's business manager. Both men pursued careers in the textile business after graduation, Hodges with Marshall Fields and Saunders with Robbins Mills.

2. Robbins was vacationing in Palm Beach, Florida, when Saunders contacted him. He agreed to visit North Carolina on his way back to New York (Aycock 1992).

3. At this time, Governor Hodges and Simpson maintained the view that the acquisition of land for the Triangle should be a for-profit undertaking.

4. Karl Robbins was an "earthy man"; his parents were Russian immigrants. Robbins probably was interested in this venture as a chance to be a "big hero in North Carolina" (Harper 1992).

5. Deposits from Robbins to Guest were recorded by Hassell W. Barton, accountant for C. M. Guest and Sons.

6. There was no formal entity called Research Triangle Park. That name has evolved over time to describe the bounded land area.

7. The first parcel of land optioned was the Rape tract (#14)—406.64 acres for $65,000; it was optioned on June 18, 1957. Then the Fletcher tract (#19)—203.24 acres for $30,000—was optioned on July 6. Third was the Stallings tract (#3), optioned on July 13—77.16 acres for $16,200. Fourth was the Gray tract (#25), optioned on July 23—35.60 acres for $6,525. And fifth was the C. H. Shipp tract (#21), optioned on July 27—70.24 acres for $10,000.

By the end of July, Robbins had sent $40,000 to Guest.

8. See, for example, the *Durham Sun*, "More Vision, More People," on

September 11. Most of the newspapers acknowledged both Governor Hodges's role and the Research Triangle Committee's work. The *Charlotte Observer* wrote on that same day in "Hodges' Research Triangle Is Quickly Gaining Maturity" that "For a one-year-old, Gov. Hodges' Research Triangle is a lusty infant." There was no mention of Romeo Guest in these articles.

In a September 11 letter to T. Y. Milburn, director of the Committee of 100 in Durham, Guest thanked him for sending maps of the Triangle area and noted as a postscript: "I fail to understand why the midwife [meaning Governor Hodges] takes all the credit for this project and the daddy [meaning Guest] is still alive. For my guidance, enlighten me, please, it might come in handy. I feel there must be some reason." Guest never understood why he was not being credited publicly for his role.

9. These new directors were Kenneth Brim; Collier Cobb, Jr., of Collier Cobb Insurance and Associates in Chapel Hill; Claude Q. Freeman of Freeman-Tate-McClinton in Charlotte; George Geoghegan of Wachovia Bank and Trust in Raleigh; George Watts Hill of Durham Bank and Trust; Alan J. Robbins (son of Karl Robbins) of Canadian Clay Products Company in Toronto; and Romeo Guest. Hill was also to represent Durham County; Geoghegan, Wake County; and Cobb, Orange County, although no Park acreage lies in Orange County.

10. Guest (1977) referred to this as another "Black Thursday," making reference to the 1929 stock market crash.

11. Robbins was on his way to Israel for a vacation when Guest approached him at the end of November for additional funds. He approved Saunders's loan by telegram on December 4 (Guest 1977). According to Guest (1977), there was nowhere else for the company to get the money it needed quickly enough.

12. At that meeting, Hassell Barton of C. M. Guest and Sons was elected assistant treasurer.

13. The minutes show that the loan from Saunders was made on December 6, although the loan agreement was signed on December 1.

14. According to Hodges (1962), three prospects that were contacted during the summer of 1957 put their plans to relocate off indefinitely, for economic reasons.

CHAPTER 5 *Dead Ends, Detours, and Redirection*

1. Pinelands Company stock certificate #4 was issued to Guest on February 4, 1958 — 120 shares at $100 par. Certificate #5 was issued to Vanore on February 10 — 50 shares at $100 par. These investments totaled $17,000, and more money would soon be invested by others.

The Pinelands Company minutes of March 20, 1958, contain a letter dated February 1 from Robbins to Pinelands. The letter requested that in return for his $275,000 investment, he wished to receive $137,500 in stock and a 5 percent debenture for $137,500, due January 15, 1978. Stock certificate #1 was issued to Robbins on February 3 for 1,375 shares at $100 par.

2. The January 31, 1958 article in the *Durham Morning Herald* was titled "Research Project Denied Blank Check for City Water."

3. The formal water contract with the City of Durham was finalized on April 21, 1958 (Jones 1978).

4. Simpson (1991) credits Arthur C. Menius for attracting this company to the area: "According to my best recollection, John Lee brought Buck Menius, physicist and head of the reactor program at N.C. State, into the fray. Buck worked for the love of it" (Simpson 1988). He also recalls the noteworthy efforts of George Watts Hill in obtaining the line of credit for the company and remembers using Astra's contract with General Electric as collateral. At that time, the local banks had never heard of lending money on the basis of research and development promises.

5. The minutes of Pinelands Company for March 20, 1958, show that it was Robbins's intention to give about two hundred acres for the Institute, when needed.

6. Ralph C. Price purchased 120 shares of stock (certificate #3) on March 13, 1958. W. E. Alexander purchased fifty shares (certificate #6) on June 28. Through the year, the original investors did invest additional funds, although certificates were not issued until December 3, 1958. Besides Robbins, North Carolinians invested a total of $169,400, including Saunders's $100,000 loan.

7. The primary lender was Wachovia Bank and Trust. Some monies were also borrowed from Durham Bank and Trust and the Bank of Chapel Hill (Aycock 1992). The loans were secured by deeds of trust held by Pinelands (Jones 1978).

8. In July, Guest had thought of liquidating the Pinelands Company. He wrote to John K. Hood, the attorney for C. M. Guest and Sons, for advice. Apparently the matter never got past this initial letter (Jones 1978).

9. Hanes's view was consistent with his previous support for Guest and his venture. According to Davis (1992), it was completely logical from the very beginning for Guest to expect money from his efforts.

10. In late September, Guest and Davis met in Raleigh. They presumably discussed the upcoming financial campaign, for on October 2, Guest wrote Davis a letter that said, "You have made me renew my faith in the Research Triangle." Guest went on to note that $2 million rather than $1.25 million would really be needed, and that "whoever gives an institute building will have no problems if he will just turn the whole thing over to me. We can take care of the interim financing, all of the details including the architecture engi-

neering, acquisition of the land and everything with no problems on the part of the benefactor or donor." The financial motive behind Guest's involvement came across very clearly in this letter.

11. For help when he was raising money, Davis called on Thomas W. Alexander. Davis's wife and Alexander's wife were cousins, and the men had been classmates at both Chapel Hill and Woodberry Forest School. Alexander was the Raleigh vice president for State Capital Life Insurance Company. Aycock (1992) remembered him as a "financial genius."

12. According to the Pinelands minutes, the liquidation was anticipated at their December 2, 1958 meeting. At that meeting the board approved a recapitalization plan and signed the Sale of Pinelands Agreement on December 3. There were 5,051 shares of Pinelands Company stock, as recorded in the stock certificate book:

| Certif. | Name | Date Issued | No. Shares |
|---|---|---|---|
| 1 | Karl Robbins | 2/3/58 | 1,375 |
| 2 | void | | |
| 3 | Ralph C. Price | 3/13/58 | 120 |
| 4 | Romeo H. Guest | 2/4/58 | 120 |
| 5 | A. A. Vanore | 2/10/58 | 50 |
| 6 | W. E. Alexander | 6/28/58 | 50 |
| 7 | W. E. Alexander | 12/3/58 | 52 |
| 8 | A. A. Vanore | 12/3/58 | 52 |
| 9 | Ralph C. Price | 12/3/58 | 125 |
| 10 | William P. Saunders | 12/3/58 | 1,000 |
| 11 | Karl Robbins | 12/3/58 | 1,982 |
| 12 | Romeo H. Guest | 12/3/58 | 125 |

Certificates #7 through #12 were issued for the record after the meeting. These stocks were given in return for previously issued debentures and notes. The 1,982 shares issued to Robbins—certificate #11—represented stock in return for the $137,500 and for his additional $55,000 loan (equaled 1,925 shares), plus accrued interest. Robbins had invested a total of $330,000 in Pinelands.

Stock certificate #13 was issued to the Research Triangle Committee, Inc., on January 2, 1959.

CHAPTER 6 *A New Beginning*

1. The minutes from the November 28, 1961 meeting of the board of directors of the Research Triangle Foundation showed total pledges of $1,737,646.76, of which $1,570,787.30 had been collected to date. One memorable contribution came from one small independent motor carrier for $4.75. All but about $30,000 was eventually collected.

2. I find it interesting that the first thing that Hodges listed was the Research Institute, given the fact that Hodges's initial enthusiasm for the Triangle project was in light of the park's potential for economic growth and development.

3. The fact of the matter was that this event came in the late evening of Hanes's life. He died that March.

Jonathan Daniels, editor of the *Raleigh News and Observer*, had long been a harsh critic of both Wachovia Bank and Robert Hanes (Aycock 1992). The *High Point Enterprise* reported on the following day that Daniels, who was seated next to Amos Kearns, was so moved by the announcement of the Hanes Building that he leaned over and said, "Amos, I'm crying." Malcolm Campbell was also at this luncheon, and he recalled that "there wasn't a dry eye in the house" (Newell 1993).

4. According to the Institute's bylaws, its ex officio governors are the president of the University of the Consolidated University of North Carolina (William Friday), the president of Duke University (Hollis Edens), and the president of the Institute (George Herbert). As recorded in the minutes, the president of the Consolidated University appointed one member from its organization (William M. Whyburn), and two members from each of the two campuses (Chancellor William B. Aycock and Alexander Heard from Chapel Hill, and Chancellor Carey H. Bostian and Walter J. Peterson from State College). The president of Duke appointed three members (Paul Gross, Marcus E. Hobbs, and Walter M. Nielsen). The two university presidents jointly appointed two members (Wilburt C. Davison from Duke and George Simpson from Chapel Hill). Twelve individuals were elected from business and industry (Robert T. Armstrong, Harry C. Carter, Clyde A. Dillon, E. Y. Floyd, P. H. Hanes, Hiram R. Hammer, George Watts Hill, Huger King, C. W. Reynolds, J. M. Wasson, Harold W. Whitcomb, and John B. Wilson).

5. The stock transfer from Pinelands to the Research Triangle Committee was also completed. Stock certificate #13 for 5,051 shares was dated January 2, 1959. The Sale of Pinelands Agreement, dated December 3, 1958, established that stockholders would be paid $117.50 per share on December 3, 1961 ($102.50 per share if paid on June 3, 1959, and so on, according to a 5 percent annual increasing schedule). Also, it was announced that the $250,000 note to Wachovia Bank and Trust had been extended until December 3, 1961.

6. Following Hanes as chairman were Gordon Gray, in 1962, and Luther Hodges, in 1965. Hodges had returned to North Carolina after serving as the U.S. Secretary of Commerce and became chairman on January 22, 1965, at an annual salary of one dollar, to be paid quarterly!

7. Davis remained president until 1981. He was not paid for this service. Fred A. Coe, Jr., followed Davis as the first paid, part-time president. Robert Leak became the first paid, full-time president in December 1985, followed by the current president, James Roberson.

8. Regarding directors, the minutes state that the board of trustees of the Consolidated University appointed Watts Hill and Thomas J. Pearsall; the board of directors of Duke University appointed Benjamin F. Few and Amos Kearns; the president of the Consolidated University (Friday) appointed William D. Carmichael; and the president of Duke University (Edens) appointed Gerhard C. Henricksen. The bylaws called for the governor (Hodges), the president of the Consolidated University, and the president of Duke University to be directors. The sixteen elected directors were John Belk; Collier Cobb, Jr.; Archie K. Davis; E. Hervey Evans; Bowman Gray; Romeo H. Guest; Robert M. Hanes; Howard Holderness; William T. Joyner; J. Spencer Love; William B. McGuire; G. Akers Moore, Jr.; R. Grady Rankin; Rueben Robertson, Sr.; William H. Ruffin; and Louis V. Sutton.

9. The so-called New Pinelands operated as Research Triangle Park, with Akers Moore as president; Pearson Stewart, vice president of planning; Elizabeth Aycock, secretary/assistant treasurer; and Thomas W. Alexander, treasurer. A separate board of nine was formed also, because Pinelands was a tax-paying subsidiary of the nonprofit Foundation (Aycock 1991). Members of the Pinelands board were Thomas Alexander; Collier Cobb, Jr.; Clyde A. Dillon; John M. Dozier; Romeo Guest; Worth A. Lutz; Akers Moore; Ralph C. Price; and Gary M. Underhill. The board would later be expanded to eleven, as noted in the minutes of January 16, to include George Geoghegan and Karl Robbins.

Although he was elected to the boards of the Foundation and of Pinelands, Guest never attended any meetings. Davis (1992) sadly recalled that the liquidation of Pinelands marked "the end of Romeo. . . . I had to go to see him. . . . He had expected always from day one that [he and his brother would get a lot of construction from this]. . . . I think it was completely reasonable, completely legitimate. . . . I had to tell him that he couldn't even sit on the board. . . . and know whom we were negotiating with and get the first shot [at the construction bid or contract]. . . . That was the saddest day I ever had."

10. According to Harper (1992), Guest was bitter about being left out of the future of the Park. In later years, when he and Guest would talk, Guest would never mention Davis's name. Harper explained, "Romeo had a tremendous ego. It had to be done his way." Patricia Nelson (1992), Guest's secretary after his retirement in 1976, agreed: "There was never any other way than his way—a perfectionist."

11. One of Stewart's responsibilities was to work closely with the local governments in planning the Park. His efforts led to the formation of the Research Triangle Regional Planning Commission (see Chapter 8).

12. This statement comes from a memorandum to file by Simpson, dated January 1959 by Aycock.

1. According to Aycock (1991), Davis preferred the word "liquidate" to the word "sell" when referring to Pinelands properties.

2. There was one bright note. Frank Soday, "a professional Charlestonian," was in Decatur. Ballentine told Little that if Soday heard of the North Carolina location, he might also speak with Chaney (Little 1992).

3. From January 1959 until August 1962, Simpson represented the University of North Carolina at Chapel Hill on the Institute's board and was also chairman of the executive committee (Herbert 1994).

4. According to Little (1992), the Chemstrand decision was the turning point in the Park's development. Others think the turning point occurred in 1965 (see Chapter 8).

5. This article speculated that Chemstrand would have an initial $5 million outlay, with an annual budget of $7 million. The following year, 185 families were moved from Decatur to the area. According to the Foundation's minutes for September 29, 1959, the Chemstrand building was expected to be 195,000 square feet, and the company anticipated employing one thousand individuals by 1965.

6. According to the minutes of the October 15, 1959, meeting of the directors of the new Pinelands Company, there were two graveyards on the Chemstrand property: "One (a white cemetery) involves some 15 graves. . . . The second graveyard is occupied by what are apparently Negro slaves and their descendants. . . . The number of graves here is estimated between 30 and 60." The board rejected the proposal to transfer the remains to a public cemetery (at a cost of $15 to exhume the remains and "place in a 12 × 16 × 30 box, ready for reburial," plus $8.62 for the reburial itself). Instead, the board agreed that the company would set aside land for its own cemetery (between the Southern Railway and U.S. 70, and north of Cornwallis Road). In the Pinelands record book there is a bill dated March 7, 1960, from Frank Pendergrass of Durham to Pinelands Company that shows "15 white bodies and 131 colored bodies. Boxes 12 × 18 × 30. From Chemstrand to Pinelands cemetery @ $25 per body." The total bill was $3,650.

7. Chemstrand actually began to occupy their facility in September 1960, before the dedication and before the Hanes Building was completed.

8. For the first time, the minutes were titled "Minutes of Directors of the Pinelands Company, Owner of the Research Triangle Park." At a July 23, 1959 meeting, the minutes were titled "Minutes of the Board of Directors of the Research Triangle Park (d.b.a. The Pinelands Company, Inc.)." The latter terminology was used thereafter, although Davis preferred and used the term New Pinelands.

9. Members of the commission were to include one representative from the governing boards of Wake, Durham, and Orange counties; one represen-

tative from each of the municipalities of Raleigh, Durham, and Chapel Hill; the mayors of the three cities; the county commissioners' board chairman from each of the three counties; and three members appointed by the governor. The first executive director was Stewart.

10. See Figure 5 in Chapter 5.

11. Davis also noted at the meeting that $300,000 would be needed for the Hanes Building, $500,000 for the Institute, and some more for other matters. He estimated that the Foundation was about $250,000 short of the amount it needed. Because the eastern part of the state had made "extremely minor contributions to the program," he planned to try to raise the additional money there.

12. There was a lot of excitement about the possibility that this missile engineering company would come to the area. According to an article in the January 11, 1959 *Winston-Salem Journal-Sentinel* entitled "Industrial 'Cape Canaveral' Looms in N.C.," Harold Clark, an economist from Columbia University, was quoted in the article as saying that the Southeast "will ultimately become the richest section of the nation again."

It should also be noted that the individual given credit for first getting ECSCO to consider the Triangle area was John D. Constabile of Wilson (*Wilson Daily Times*, January 12, 1959).

13. The first mention of Shea's hiring is in the August 6, 1959 minutes of Pinelands. He was simply presented at that meeting as the new executive vice president. No vote was ever taken. According to Aycock (1992), this was Moore's "typical after-the-fact management style."

14. See Figure 4 in Chapter 4.

15. The Sale of Pinelands Agreement set forth a price schedule of early redemption of the stock.

16. The cost of the Hanes Building was $321,000.

17. Allied Chemical held an option to purchase land, but it was never exercised.

18. The minutes of the Board of Directors of the Foundation from July 27, 1960, refer to "Company X" being interested in about four hundred acres. In the August 18 executive committee meeting, Company X was referred to as "Minute Maid" for confidentiality. In other Foundation correspondence, Minute Maid is revealed to be General Electric. The company eventually purchased land in the Park in 1980.

19. Again, the announcement of the U.S. Forest Service laboratory underscored that the development of the Park would be a slow process. George Simpson began negotiations with the Forest Service shortly after becoming director. At the Foundation's August 6, 1959 meeting, his original commitment to donate twenty-five acres of land for their laboratory was renewed by the Foundation's board.

20. Currie had previously been associated with both Union Carbide and Babcock and Wilcox.

21. The 1962–63 financial statement for the Foundation showed the $1.3 million liability to the banks and insurance companies that had loaned it money the year before, and it showed net income of just under $4,000.

22. The ground-breaking for the center took place on January 8, 1965.

23. Ned Huffman was previously the division manager at Southern Bell Telephone and Telegraph Company in Raleigh.

24. Herbert (1993) realized this level of commitment even before accepting the position of president of the Research Triangle Institute. Recalling his early visits to the Triangle, he said, "I sensed a feeling of enthusiasm, confidence, and commitment on the part of everybody I talked to."

## CHAPTER 8 *Ceasing to Be Pioneers*

1. The Research Triangle Park post office was originally set up in the basement of the North Carolina Science and Technology building.

2. In a May 17, 1965 memorandum, Chanlett noted that on June 14, 1961, President Kennedy's budget was modified to include funds for site acquisition and planning for an environmental health center. A Committee on Environmental Health Problems was appointed on August 1 to assist with the planning, and Duke University's Paul Gross chaired the committee.

3. One readable and accurate history of these events appeared in the *Chapel Hill Weekly* on January 10, 1965.

4. Gross also favored this location because of its proximity to a large population of research scientists, according to an article that appeared in the *Washington Post* on September 8, 1964.

5. According to Aycock (1992), Luther Hodges and Celebrezze had become "fishing buddies" when Hodges was U.S. secretary of commerce. The North Carolina delegation was certainly well connected.

6. Aycock (1992) remembered that he would stay at the rather "modest" Cadillac Motel on Highway 70 in order to remain inconspicuous.

7. According to Herbert (1993), "with the IBM decision, the Park had achieved critical mass and . . . from that point on the role which the Institute had played in giving credibility to the Park" diminished in its relative importance.

8. The *Raleigh News and Observer* reported on June 21, 1965, that J. B. Rhine, a parapsychologist from Duke University who intended to build an "Institute on the Nature of Man" in the Park, had had a change of plans. This cancellation was perhaps the Park's only negative event that year. Aycock (1992) recalled the day Rhine first visited the Foundation's board to describe his institute. Luther Hodges, who had recently become the board's chairman,

told Rhine (in typical Hodges fashion) that the Foundation would be happy to have him in the Park, but "if you did research on the nature of women it would be much more interesting."

9. Hodges had known Erwin Meltzer, head of Beaunit, for a long time. Still, this acquisition took years of courting.

10. On July 4, 1965, the *Durham Herald* published a drawing captioned "Wooing Industry Is Big Business." It illustrated, in 1965 dollars, the economic impact of the Research Triangle Park. For every 100 new employees in the Park, there would be 359 additional jobs in the area, 91 new children enrolling in schools, $229,000 in new bank deposits, 3 new retail stores opening, 97 new automobiles being registered, and $331,000 in additional retail sales.

Over the past years, Archie Davis has been called upon time and time again to ensure the lasting success of the Park. Davis (1992) remembered one such event in particular. Someone called him on a Saturday night in June 1985 and told him that during the next week, the Durham delegation would introduce a bill in the state General Assembly; this bill would extend Durham's city limits to include the Park. Davis went to Durham on Sunday to get Kenneth Royall's advice on how to handle this unfortunate situation. Royall advised Davis to meet with the Durham delegation before the bill was introduced. Davis followed the advice and told the Durham delegation that "if this is done . . . it will destroy the integrity of the Research Triangle Park. The Park was built on integrity and trust, and here the City of Durham is going to swallow it up." Receiving "no satisfaction" from the Durham legislators, Davis went to the General Assembly committee on Monday evening and told them the history of how the money was raised and how the Park was built. He told them that Winston-Salem began its $1.25 million project with $450,000 (significantly more than was collected from Durham). "If my people [Winston-Salem] knew then that . . . the City of Durham was going to take it over, [no money would have been given]. . . . I could hardly contain my voice." On June 24, 1985, House Bill 926, "An Act to Authorize Counties to Establish Research and Production Service Districts," was signed and ratified. Not only did this bill ensure that no Park land could be annexed by Durham City; it also legislated a mechanism for providing services to the Park.

# BIBLIOGRAPHY

*All correspondence cited in the text but not listed here is located in the Research Triangle Foundation archives. Also, unless otherwise stated, all interviews were performed by the author.*

Alexander, John. 1993. February 3 telephone interview.
Aycock, Elizabeth. 1989. "History—'The Research Triangle.' " Mimeographed article dated October 19.
———. 1991–94. Interviews at the Research Triangle Foundation, Research Triangle Park, N.C.
Bostian, Carey H. 1991. July 11 interview at Bostian's home in Chapel Hill, N.C.
Brown, Lamont. 1981. July 13 interview by William P. Saunders at Brown's office in Southern Pines, N.C.
Caldwell, John T. 1991. October 4 interview at Caldwell's home in Raleigh, N.C.
Campbell, Malcolm E., and William A. Newell. 1954. "A Proposal for the Development of an Industrial Research Center in North Carolina." Mimeographed article dated December 27.
Case, Phyllis Branch. 1960. June 1 letter to George Simpson.
———. 1991a. September 30 telephone interview.
———. 1991b. October 14 letter to Albert N. Link.
Cherry, R. Gregg. 1946. "Research for the Commonwealth." In *Research and*

*Regional Welfare*, edited by Robert E. Coker. Chapel Hill: University of North Carolina Press. 3–15.

Coker, Robert E. 1946. *Research and Regional Welfare*. Chapel Hill: University of North Carolina Press.

Colvard, Dean W. 1986. Transcript of March 7 interview with Romeo H. Guest, Southern Pines, N.C.

Davis, Archibald K. 1992. March 4 interview at Davis's home in Winston-Salem, N.C.

Davis, Nancy. 1984. Transcript of April 11 interview with Romeo H. Guest at the Country Club of North Carolina in Pinehurst, N.C.

Elmore, Cindy. 1983. Transcript of May 12 interview with Romeo H. Guest at the Country Club of North Carolina in Pinehurst, N.C.

Franco, Michael R. 1985. "Key Success Factors for University-Affiliated Research Parks: A Comparative Analysis." Ph.D. diss., University of Rochester.

Friday, William C. 1993. March 29 interview at the Kenan Center, University of North Carolina at Chapel Hill.

Guest, Romeo H. 1976. Transcript of November 30 meeting at the Carolina Inn in Chapel Hill, N.C.

———. 1977. "The Story of the Research Triangle from 'Think-Up through 'Start-Up." Mimeographed article dated August 31.

———. 1978. Transcript of May 15 meeting at the Carolina Inn in Chapel Hill, N.C.

———. 1979. Transcript of November 9 meeting at Lamont Brown's office in Southern Pines, N.C.

———. 1980. Transcript of January 27 meeting at Lamont Brown's office in Southern Pines, N.C.

———. 1981. Transcript of May 9 meeting at Lamont Brown's office in Southern Pines, N.C.

———. 1983. Transcript of April 4 meeting at Clifton Blue's office in Aberdeen, N.C.

Guest, William S. 1960. "Research Triangle Park." Master's thesis, University of North Carolina at Chapel Hill.

Hamilton, William B. 1966. "The Research Triangle of North Carolina: A Study in Leadership for the Common Weal." *South Atlantic Quarterly* 65, no. 2 (Spring): 254–78.

Harper, Walter W. 1960. March 31 letter to Phyllis Branch.

———. 1991. June 21 interview at the University of North Carolina at Greensboro.

———. 1992. November 6 interview at the University of North Carolina at Greensboro.

Herbert, George R. 1993. August 9 interview at the Research Triangle Institute, Research Triangle Park, N.C.

————. 1994. April 28 letter to William F. Little.

Hill, George Watts. 1991. July 9 interview at Hill's office in Durham, N.C.

Hobbs, Marcus E. 1982. "The Research Triangle of North Carolina: An Example of University, Corporate, and Government Working Together for the Common Good." Paper presented at Florida State University, March 5–6.

————. 1991. October 31 interview at Hobbs's office at Duke University, Durham, N.C.

Hodges, Luther H. 1962. *Businessman in the Statehouse: Six Years as Governor of North Carolina.* Chapel Hill: University of North Carolina Press.

Jones, Mary Virginia. 1978. "A 'Golden Triangle' of Research: Romeo Holland Guest—His Conception and Involvement in the Development of the Research Triangle Park." Master's thesis, University of North Carolina at Chapel Hill.

Larrabee, Charles X. 1992. *Many Missions: Research Triangle Institute's First 31 Years.* Research Triangle Park, N.C.: Research Triangle Institute.

Little, William F. 1989. "The Research Triangle Park of North Carolina—A U.S. Science City." Paper presented at the Corporation Associates of Pacific Basin Societies, Honolulu, Hawaii, December 19.

————. 1992. February 10 interview at the University of North Carolina at Chapel Hill.

————. 1993. October 6 interview at the University of North Carolina at Chapel Hill.

Nelson, Patricia P. 1992. November 8 telephone interview.

Newell, William A. "Miscellaneous Papers Pertaining to the Research Triangle." Undated file prepared by Newell in the Research Triangle Foundation archives.

Newell, William A. 1989. "Statement of William A. Newell Relative to His Involvement in the Founding of the Research Triangle and Research Triangle Park of North Carolina." Mimeographed article dated October 19.

————. 1992. December 12 telephone interview.

————. 1993. July 18 letter to Albert N. Link.

Pinelands Company. Various dates. Minutes and correspondence.

Reagan, Alice Elizabeth. 1987. *North Carolina State University: A Narrative History.* Ann Arbor, Mich.: Edward Brothers, Inc.

Research Triangle Committee. Various dates. Minutes and correspondence.

Research Triangle Foundation. Various dates. Minutes and correspondence.

Simpson, George L. 1957a. "Memorandum on the Research Triangle Program for Members and Working Committee." January 18.

————. 1957b. "The Research Triangle of North Carolina." Mimeographed speech delivered at the Faculty Club at the University of North Carolina at Chapel Hill, February 5.

————. 1988. "Comments on the Research Triangle of North Carolina." Mimeographed article.

———. 1991. November 19 interview at Simpson's home in Atlanta, Ga.

———. 1993a. May 14 telephone interview.

———. 1993b. May 18 letter to Albert N. Link.

———. 1993c. May 31 letter to Albert N. Link.

———. 1993d. June 13 letter to Albert N. Link.

Spivey, Walter A. 1956. "An Analysis of Per Capita Income in the States and Regions of the U.S., 1929–1953." Ph.D. diss., University of North Carolina at Chapel Hill.

Stewart, Pearson H. 1993. March 29 interview at Stewart's home in Chapel Hill, N.C.

Vogel, Ezra F. 1985. *Comeback Case by Case: Building the Resurgence of American Business.* New York: Simon and Schuster.

Williams, Edith W. 1948. *Research in Southern Regional Development.* Richmond: Dietz Press.

Wilson, Louis R. 1967. *The Research Triangle of North Carolina: A Notable Achievement in University, Governmental, and Industrial Cooperative Development.* Chapel Hill: Colonial Press.

York, J. Willie. 1993. February 2 telephone interview.

# INDEX

A page reference in italics denotes an illustration; *n* with a page reference denotes a note. Government agencies are entered under the appropriate jurisdiction, e.g., North Carolina State Highway Commission; United States Internal Revenue Service.

Program and Plans Subcommittee
(Working Committee), 28–29,
30, 34
"A Proposal for the Development of an
Industrial Research Center in
North Carolina" (Campbell and
Newell), 16, 19–20, 117nn 27–30
Pullen, A. M., 55
Purks, Harris, 16, 26

Raleigh, 121n 7, 130n 9
Raleigh Chamber of Commerce, 121n 6
Raleigh-Durham Airport, 15, 19, 87
*Raleigh News and Observer*, 14, 127n 3
on environmental health center, 88
on R. Guest, 118n 33
on library budgets, 123n 22
on Rhine, 131n 8
on Simpson, 121n 2
on university facilities, 29
*Raleigh Times*, 59
Raleigh Tractor and Truck Company
(firm), 35
Randino, Andy, 90
Rankin, Edward, 63
Rankin, Grady, 30, 119n 7, 128n 8
Rape tract, 54, 123n 7
Rawls, Guy W., 121n 18
Reedy Creek Park, 45
"Research and Industry as a Factor in
Southern Development" (Fries),
116n 17
"The Research Triangle Committee — A
Final Report of Activities"
(Simpson), 76
Research Triangle Committee, Inc.
financing efforts of, 64–65, 121n 7
incorporation of, 33–34, 77–78
meetings of
Jan. 18, 1957, 42, 44, 45, 48, 51
Oct. 22, 1958, 69
Jan. 2, 1959, 74
membership of, 121n 19
newspapers and, 124n 8
offices of, 37

policies of, 38
Program and Plans Subcommittee
recommendation on, 28
promotional efforts of, 59–60
"The Research Triangle of North
Carolina," 40–41
stock certificate issued to, 126n 12
*See also* Research Triangle
Foundation
Research Triangle Development
Committee (Working Committee)
establishment of, 27
executive search of, 29–31, 120n 15
meetings of
Jan. 26, 1955, 30
July 21, 1955, 27–28
Oct. 20, 1955, 29–30
Mar. 18, 1956, 30
Jan. 18, 1957, 42, 44, 45, 48
membership of, 108, 121n 19
minutes of, 120n 10
Research Triangle Development
Committee (Working Committee)
Inventory Preparation
Subcommittee, 28, 30
Research Triangle Development
Committee (Working Committee)
Program and Plans Subcommittee,
28–29, 30, 34
Research Triangle Development
Council, 27, 30–31
Research Triangle Foundation, 73,
76, 88
Environmental Health Sciences
Center and, 89, 90
finances of, 83, 84, 126n 1, 130n 11,
131n 21
"Minute Maid" and, 130n 18
mortgage burned by, 91
name change of, 74
Pinelands liquidated by. *See under*
Pinelands Company
Triangle Service Center and, 92
U.S. Bureau of Public Roads and, 82
*See also* Research Triangle
Committee, Inc.